P9-DHP-130

Computer and Network
Security in Higher Education

Mark Luker
Rodney Petersen, Editors

Computer and Network Security in Higher Education

EDUCAUSE

Leadership Strategies No. 8

JOSSEY-BASS
A Wiley Imprint
www.josseybass.com

Published by Jossey-Bass
A Wiley Imprint
989 Market Street, San Francisco, CA 94103-1741   www.josseybass.com

This book is part of the Jossey-Bass Higher and Adult Education Series.

Jossey-Bass books and products are available through most bookstores. To contact
Jossey-Bass directly call our Customer Care Department within the U.S. at 800-956-7739,
outside the U.S. at 317-572-3986 or fax 317-572-4002.

Jossey-Bass also publishes its books in a variety of electronic formats. Some content that
appears in print may not be available in electronic books.

Library of Congress Cataloging-in-Publication Data

　　Computer and network security in higher education / edited by Mark Luker and
Rodney Petersen.
　　　　p. cm. — (EDUCAUSE leadership strategies ; no. 8)
　　　Includes bibliographical references and index.
　　ISBN 0-7879-6666-5 (alk. paper)
　　　　1. Universities and colleges—Computer networks—Security measures—
United States. 2. Computer security—United States. 3. Education, Higher—
Effect of technological innovations on—United States. I. Luker, Mark A., 1947-
II. Petersen, Rodney J. III. EDUCAUSE (Association) IV. Series.
LB2395.7.C65 2004
005.8—dc21   2003014534

Printed in the United States of America
FIRST EDITION
PB Printing　　10 9 8 7 6 5 4 3 2 1

The EDUCAUSE Leadership Strategies series addresses critical themes related to information technology that will shape higher education in the years to come. The series is intended to make a significant contribution to the knowledge academic leaders can draw upon to chart a course for their institutions into a technology-based future. Books in the series offer practical advice and guidelines to help campus leaders develop action plans to further that end. The series is developed by EDUCAUSE and published by Jossey-Bass. The sponsorship of PricewaterhouseCoopers LLP makes it possible for EDUCAUSE to distribute complimentary copies of books in the series to more than 1,800 EDUCAUSE member institutions, organizations, and corporations.

EDUCAUSE

EDUCAUSE is a nonprofit association with offices in Boulder, Colorado, and Washington, D.C. The association's mission is to advance higher education by promoting the intelligent use of information technology. EDUCAUSE activities include an educational program of conferences, workshops, seminars, and institutes; a variety of print and on-line publications; strategic/policy initiatives such as the National Learning Infrastructure Initiative, the Net@EDU program, and the EDUCAUSE Center for Applied Research; and extensive Web-based information services.

EDUCAUSE
- provides professional development opportunities for those involved with planning for, managing, and using information technologies in colleges and universities
- seeks to influence policy by working with leaders in the education, corporate, and government sectors who have a stake in the transformation of higher education through information technologies
- enables the transfer of leading-edge approaches to information technology management and use that are developed and shared through EDUCAUSE policy and strategy initiatives
- provides a forum for dialogue between information resources professionals and campus leaders at all levels
- keeps members informed about information technology innovations, strategies, and practices that may affect their campuses, identifying and researching the most pressing issues

Current EDUCAUSE membership includes more than 1,800 campuses, organizations, and corporations. For up-to-date information about EDUCAUSE programs, initiatives, and services, visit the association's Web site at www.educause.edu, send e-mail to info@educause.edu, or call 303-449-4430.

PRICEWATERHOUSE COOPERS

PricewaterhouseCoopers is a leading provider of professional services to institutions of higher education, serving a full range of educational institutions—from small colleges to large public and private universities to educational companies.

PricewaterhouseCoopers (www.pwcglobal.com) is the world's largest professional services organization, drawing on the knowledge and skills of more than 150,000 people in 150 countries to help clients solve complex business problems and measurably enhance their ability to build value, manage risk, and improve performance in an Internet-enabled world.

PricewaterhouseCoopers refers to the member firms of the worldwide PricewaterhouseCoopers organization.

Contents

Foreword

College and university executives are increasingly aware of the importance of computer and network security in their institutions. The *Chronicle of Higher Education* and other national and local media regularly report on information security incidents at colleges and universities. A letter was sent in February 2003 to all college and university presidents from the president of the American Council on Education stressing the importance and urgency of cybersecurity in higher education and the need for campus leadership and engagement (www.acenet.edu/washington/letters/2003/03march/cyber.cfm).

Has this awareness been translated into institutionwide policy, well-understood authority, and adequate resources to secure campus information technology resources? Are campus information security officers employing and sharing effective practices and solutions? Is higher education doing its part in securing the Internet, which is increasingly a mission-critical tool to education, business, government, and national security?

The EDUCAUSE/Internet2 Computer and Network Security Task Force was established in the summer of 2000 to address these issues. One impetus for this collaborative effort was the widely publicized *distributed denial-of-service* (DDOS) attacks that had occurred earlier that year on such key Internet sites as Amazon.com, CNN, eBay, and Yahoo. These attacks were traced to insecure computers at two universities. Another was the realization that Internet2, higher education's flagship networking initiative, needed to ensure that high-performance connections and next-generation collaborative applications did not carry with them advanced security risks. Aided immeasurably by a grant from the National Science Foundation, the security task force has developed awareness and best practice seminars, created an information resources Web site, launched an annual conference for campus information security professionals, supported establishment of the Research and Educational Networking Information Sharing and Analysis Center (REN-ISAC) at Indiana University, and orchestrated higher education's contribution to the recently published *National Strategy to Secure Cyberspace* (www.securecyberspace.gov).

Two observations from the *National Strategy* bear repeating here. First, colleges and universities are targeted for exploitation because they possess vast amounts of computing power and because they allow relatively open access to those resources. This open access takes many forms: weak Internet gateway firewalls, lest essential interinstitutional collaboration be impeded; minimal standards for attaching and configuring computers and other devices to networks; a long-standing commitment to remote access and emerging deployment of wireless access; and a culture of innovation and trust. Second, much of the computing power at colleges and universities—servers and workstations in research laboratories, desktops and laptops in wired residence halls—is not managed by IT professionals, if it is managed at all. These are not hypothetical vulnerabilities—high-profile security breaches have occurred in several universities, exposing student, employee, and patient records.

Creation of the REN-ISAC, inclusion of the higher education sector in the *National Strategy*, and establishment and funding of information security offices in numerous universities and colleges are all positive signs, but much remains to be done. Too many software and hardware products are delivered with insecure configurations or with coding errors that can be exploited to gain unauthorized access. Too many of our academic colleagues believe that "no one would be interested in my fruit fly database," not realizing that the computing power of the underlying server, not the data, is often the resource prized by intruders. Too few of our IT organizations have the authorization, expertise, and staff resources to scan their networks for vulnerabilities, even as the frequency and sophistication of hostile network scans increase. In addition, just as we are facing up to the magnitude of these problems, most of our institutions are facing budget difficulties.

Nearly three years after the first large-scale DDOS, an even more potent attack, the so-called "SQL Slammer," hit the Internet in early 2003. From an unknown origin, this attack proliferated worldwide around the Internet within ten minutes, penetrating tens of thousands of computers with vulnerable software (that is, software to which available patches had not been applied) and causing, by some measures, a 20 percent reduction in Internet accessibility. Colleges and universities responding to a task force survey reported that 75 percent were affected, with some effectively unable to access the Internet for hours—or days—either because their systems had become overloaded or because their Internet service providers had disconnected them to stop the rogue traffic emanating from the penetrated systems.

Every college and university needs a strategy to secure its information resources, a top-level commitment to establish and enforce policies, and an organization that can provide leadership, expertise, and real-time incident response. We must protect our intellectual property and critical records, the privacy of our constituents, and the integrity of our systems, lest they be used against us or our neighbors on the Internet. And we must accomplish this without sacrificing our mission and core values.

The expert contributors to this volume address all of these issues and more. They write from long experience on the forefront of cybersecurity and from heated discussions about the most technically viable, most cost-effective, or most culturally appropriate approaches to securing our college and university networks. They have been, and will continue to be, key contributors to the ongoing work of the security task force. We hope you will join us in this important national effort and will find the resources contained in this book of assistance as you seek to improve computer and network security at your campus.

Daniel Updegrove, co-chair of the EDUCAUSE/Internet2 Computer and Network Security Task Force and vice president for Information Technology, The University of Texas at Austin

Gordon Wishon, co-chair of the EDUCAUSE/Internet2 Computer and Network Security Task Force and chief information officer and associate vice president/associate provost, University of Notre Dame

Preface

You don't have to look very far to find a president, chief information officer, or public relations director in higher education who can
recount a recent incident in which information security was compromised at his or her institution. The stories often contain similar
themes: a wide range of problems for victims whose data are lost or
exposed, bad publicity for the institution, threats of lawsuits and
legal liability, and significant expenditure of energy and resources
in recovery and cleanup. Contributing factors often, but not always,
include careless behavior by employees or students, faulty system
administration by overworked and inadequately trained personnel,
inadequate preventive measures, absence of risk analyses and testing for vulnerabilities, outdated policies and procedures, and insufficient supervision or leadership. With such a bleak outlook, is there
any hope for a remedy or possible cure?

Although the obstacles and challenges for improving computer
and network security in higher education may seem daunting, we
have reason for optimism and hope. Significant progress has been
made in the past few years by a number of colleges and universities,
many of which will be highlighted in this book. This book is
designed to provide both a conceptual framework and a launching
point for the development of comprehensive information security
programs to address risk factors such as these in the college and university environment.

Higher Education and the Protection of Critical Infrastructure

The information and communication resources of the Internet, now considered a critical part of the national infrastructure, are indispensable to research and education. The educational mission of most campuses now requires direct access to computing and the Internet for every student. Issues of student turnover, evolving technology, technical diversity, decentralized management, funding, and the sheer size of the populations involved present special challenges for cybersecurity in the "wired" as well as the "wireless" campus.

Higher education and officials in the White House and the new Department of Homeland Security are understandably nervous about the vulnerabilities in computer systems and networks on which many of our critical infrastructures depend. There is also recognition of the interdependence among government, industry, and higher education in the reliability and performance of computer networks (Computer Science and Telecommunications Board, 2003). Therefore, a national effort was initiated following the attacks on America on September 11, 2001, to examine cybersecurity along with the physical, chemical, and biological threats to our homeland.

The resulting *National Strategy to Secure Cyberspace* was signed by President George W. Bush in February 2003. According to the *National Strategy*, "The purpose of this document is to engage and empower Americans to secure the portions of cyberspace that they own, operate, control, or with which they interact" (*National Strategy*, 2003, p. vii). A cover letter from the president to the American people summarized the issue and corresponding national policy as follows: "In the past few years, threats in cyberspace have risen dramatically. The policy of the United States is to protect against the debilitating disruption of the operation of information systems for critical infrastructures and, thereby, help to protect the people, economy, and national security of the United States. We must act to reduce our vulnerabilities to these threats before they can be exploited to damage the cyber systems supporting our Nation's critical infrastructures and ensure that such disruptions of cyberspace are infrequent, of minimal duration, manageable, and cause the least damage possible" (*National Strategy*, 2003).

The EDUCAUSE/Internet2 Computer and Network Security Task Force, representing higher education, participated in the development of the *National Strategy* directly with staff from the White House and other federal agencies. One of the outcomes of this recent engagement between the security task force and key players within the federal government is government recognition that higher education plays an important role in the cybersecurity of America. Through its core mission of teaching and learning, it is the main source of our future leaders, innovators, and technical workforce. Through research, it is the source of much of our new knowledge and subsequent technologies. And finally, colleges and universities operate some of the world's largest collections of computers and high-speed networks.

Any successful national response to the threat of cyber terrorism must include steps to strengthen and protect the security of college and university networks and information resources. Institutions of higher education have a responsibility to ensure that their computing and networking facilities are not used to launch attacks on critical infrastructure beyond the campus.

Higher education represents a great national resource with which to explore solutions and develop strategies for cybersecurity in an open and free society. The values of higher education are, in the end, those of the nation. The computers and networks of higher education represent, in many cases, the emerging systems of the future. Successful security implementations in higher education can serve as guideposts for related developments in the nation at large.

The final version of the *National Strategy* encourages colleges and universities "to secure their cyber systems by establishing some or all of the following as appropriate":

1. One or more information sharing and analysis centers to deal with cyberattacks and vulnerabilities
2. An on-call point-of-contact to Internet service providers and law enforcement officials in the event that the school's IT systems are discovered to be launching cyberattacks
3. Model guidelines empowering chief information officers (CIOs) to address cybersecurity
4. One or more sets of best practices for IT security
5. Model user awareness programs and materials (*National Strategy*, 2003, pp. 25, 41)

The Commitment to Cybersecurity in Higher Education

Higher education has completed a number of significant, concrete steps to move forward with cybersecurity on a national basis. The locus of discussion and planning has been the EDUCAUSE/Internet2 Computer and Network Security Task Force, organized in the summer of 2000. In early 2002, the task force drafted a five-part *Framework for Action* that pledged the following:

1. Make IT security a higher and more visible priority in higher education.
2. Do a better job with existing security tools, including revision of institutional policies.
3. Design, develop, and deploy improved security for future research and education networks.
4. Raise the level of security collaboration among higher education, industry, and government.
5. Integrate higher education work on security into the broader national effort to strengthen critical infrastructure.

The *Framework for Action* was ratified by the American Council on Education and the remaining members of the Higher Education Information Technology Alliance in April 2002. It was then presented to Richard Clarke, formerly special advisor to the president for cyberspace security, when he addressed Networking 2002, an annual national policy meeting for campus information technology leaders. The *Framework for Action* continues to guide the efforts of the task force, and the first three items are addressed in considerable measure by the authors of this book.

Overview of the Book

The chapters in this book are designed to give readers a broad view of the most important ingredients to a successful information security program. Each of the chapters covers topics on which entire books could have been written. Therefore, the content identified and included in this book is designed to provide higher education leadership and management with the necessary overview and stimuli to improve the state of computer and network security at their own campus. The book's authors, however, are practitioners whose experience and insights will also inform IT security professionals responsible for program implementation.

The first chapter examines the unique mission of higher education and values of the academic community. There is sometimes concern that efforts to improve computer and network security will compromise important academic values. There is the mistaken belief that the introduction of better security practices and new institutional policies will be at the expense of privacy or will result in loss of academic freedom. This chapter introduces general principles established during a workshop sponsored by the National Science Foundation that should guide efforts to improve computer and network security in the academic environment.

Initiating a program to improve the security of college and university computers and networks can be both intimidating and overwhelming. The second chapter provides a road map for organizing to improve security. The author discusses the challenges of finding resources and establishing leadership for security and the evolving role of the IT security officer.

The third chapter describes one of the first steps for improving IT security in a college or university setting: conducting a security assessment and risk analysis. Security assessments may be conducted by using internal resources or by employing an external organization that specializes in vulnerability testing and other techniques that measure the extent of an institution's exposure to known threats. This information can be combined with corresponding estimates of potential institutional losses to yield a prioritized list of preventive actions. The author describes a successful technique, Security Targeting and Analysis of Risks (STAR), used at the Virginia Polytechnic Institute and State University.

Another important aspect of risk analysis is consideration of legal liability that could result from a security incident. The fourth chapter explores the potential for a college or university to be found negligent in its application of information security. The lack of legal precedent and contemporary experiences with actual IT security incidents mean that there is little direct evidence for making informed choices about the level of risk to tolerate and the payoff that comes from instituting preventive measures. It is inevitable that a combination of incidents of legal liability, based on issues of negligence and business continuity among other things, and new government regulation will make attention to legal issues an important consideration.

Information technology has become an issue of strategic importance for colleges and universities. Chapter Five describes the importance of including cybersecurity in planning and the necessity of developing appropriate institutional policies and procedures. The authors provide an overview of policy development to address the increasing complexity of security issues.

Chapter Six describes how the development of a security architecture and use of an array of technology tools can enhance the security of campus systems. College and university computer systems and networks have evolved in response to innovations and perceived needs of the education and research communities. However, the evolution has resulted in IT infrastructures that are seldom coherent and rarely cost effective, where attention to security has often been an afterthought. An opportunity for a renewed focus on IT security awaits us as colleges and universities attempt to overhaul their network and application architectures, and focus on strategies for life-cycle replacement of hardware and leveraged software licensing.

Finally, experts in computer and network security usually cite people as both the most significant source of IT security problems and the most important element of any program that seeks to improve security. Therefore, no treatment of computer and network security would be complete without a chapter that describes the importance of education and awareness in an overall campus information security program. As discussed in Chapter Seven, short-term efforts must be made to raise the awareness of senior executives, IT professionals, and end users regarding the severity and criticality of IT security issues. Long-term solutions will require persistence and ongoing professional development of system administrators and other IT professionals.

Tactics for improving computer and network security will evolve and change along with the technology over time. Accordingly, the authors and editors recognize the importance of providing readers with general information that is likely to survive the test of time and a sufficient number of specific suggestions to stimulate near-term campus initiatives. Each of the topics can benefit from the sharing of effective practices and solutions on an ongoing basis. For this reason the EDUCAUSE/Internet2 Computer and Network Security Task Force will continue to promote information sharing and identification of useful resources through its Web site, periodic publications, and outreach at conferences and other professional development events. For more information, consult www.educause.edu/security.

October 2003   Mark Luker
                                                  Rodney Petersen

References

Computer Science and Telecommunications Board, National Research Council. *Cyber Security Today and Tomorrow: Pay Now or Pay Later*. Washington, D.C.: National Academy Press, 2003.

National Strategy to Secure Cyberspace. [www.securecyberspace.gov]. Feb. 2003.

Acknowledgments

A book of this kind is made possible through the expertise, hard work, and dedication of authors, the leadership of the EDUCAUSE/Internet2 Computer and Network Security Task Force, and the EDUCAUSE staff. We would like to thank the authors for their insights and unique perspectives. We are also grateful for their devotion of time and energy—above and beyond other job duties—that will provide higher education executives and IT professionals with critical information that will support campus efforts to improve computer and network security.

We want to acknowledge the wisdom and underlying contributions of the leadership of the Security Task Force and participants of the security workshops funded by the National Science Foundation. The workshop discussions helped formulate many of the ideas contained within Chapter One ("IT Security and Academic Values"). The Security Task Force leadership continues to provide expertise and direction in the overall strategy and agenda for cybersecurity on behalf of higher education.

Finally, we are also indebted to the support and assistance received from Cynthia Golden of EDUCAUSE. Cynthia supported the editors by working directly with some of the authors and carefully proofreading multiple drafts. We are grateful for her dedication and help with this project, in particular, and appreciate her continuing support of the Security Task Force in her role as executive director of professional development.

The Authors

Mark Luker is vice president of EDUCAUSE, where he heads the Washington, D.C.-based policy program as well as Net@EDU. He is a leader in the EDUCAUSE/Internet2 Computer and Network Security Task Force, the Higher Education Bridge Certification Authority, and the National Science Foundation (NSF) program in Advanced Networking with Minority Serving Institutions. Previously, he was program director for advanced networking and the Next Generation Internet project at the NSF. Luker also served as chief information officer at the University of Wisconsin-Madison and as a faculty member and acting dean at the University of Minnesota Duluth. He received his doctorate from the University of California, Berkeley.

Rodney Petersen is the project director for the EDUCAUSE/Internet2 Computer and Network Security Task Force and a policy analyst with EDUCAUSE. He previously served as director of IT Policy and Planning in the Office of the Vice President and CIO at the University of Maryland. He was the founder of Project NEThics at the University of Maryland, which was established to educate the community about responsible use of computing resources and enforce acceptable use policies. Petersen has authored numerous publications and is a frequent speaker on the topics of information security, copyright, privacy, and institutional policy development for the appropriate use of information technology in higher education. He received his law degree from Wake Forest University.

Mark Bruhn is chief IT security and policy officer at Indiana University. In this role, he advises the administration on technology deployment, usage, and security issues, and directs the efforts of the University IT Policy Office and the University IT Security Office. He is also associate director of the Indiana University Center for Applied Cybersecurity Research (CACR), and recently was appointed acting director of the Research and Educational Networking Information Sharing and Analysis Center (REN-ISAC) based at Indiana University. Bruhn is a member of the EDUCAUSE/Internet2 Computer and Network Security Task Force. He has a bachelor's degree in computer science from Park College and is a Certified Information Systems Security Professional.

Randy Marchany is director of the Virginia Tech Security Testing Lab. He is also the coordinator of VA-CIRT and a member of the White House Working Group for Critical Infrastructure Security. He is the author of numerous computer security documents, including the standard acceptable use policy used in the Virginia State University system, is co-author of the FBI/SANS Institute's "Top 10/20 Internet Security Vulnerabilities" list, and is currently working on a SANS publication on Internet security audit programs. Marchany has taught professional development seminars and has spoken at both national and international conferences on a variety of security topics. He is the recipient of the SANS Institute's Security Technology Leadership Award for 2000.

Diana Oblinger is the executive director of higher education for Microsoft Corporation and adjunct professor at North Carolina State University. Previously, she served as the vice president for information resources and the chief information officer for the sixteen-campus University of North Carolina system. Oblinger has been a consultant and senior fellow for the EDUCAUSE Center for Applied Research, led the Institute for Academic Technology for IBM, and served on the faculty at Michigan State University and the University of Missouri–Columbia. A frequent keynote speaker, Oblinger has authored and edited numerous books and publications, including the award-winning *What Business Wants from Higher Education*. She is a graduate of Iowa State University.

Shirley Payne is director for security coordination and policy at the University of Virginia. In this capacity she focuses on the continuous enhancement of information technology policies and security of the university's diverse and decentralized computing environment. She works across the university to formulate policies, assess security risk, establish strategic direction, and provide security education and training and related activities. She has thirty-two years of experience in information technology, most of which has been in higher education. She holds a bachelor's degree in computer science from Winthrop University and a master's degree in management information systems from the University of Virginia.

Jeff Recor is president and CEO of the Olympus Security Group, Inc., where he advises clients on the topics of security strategy, return on investment (ROI), and risk mitigation. He has more than eighteen years of experience in the security field, including positions as director of Nortel Networks' Global Professional Services Security Practice and president of the Sargon Group, Inc. An adjunct professor at Walsh College, Recor is the author of three books and numerous articles on this topic. He is currently assisting the White House on infrastructure protection and security research issues. He is a graduate of Michigan State University.

Nancy E. Tribbensee is deputy general counsel at Arizona State University. She advises the university in the areas of intellectual property, technology transfer, research, student affairs, free speech, risk management, and computer use and security. She is a member of the National Association of College and University Attorneys (NACUA) and serves on the NACUA Publications Committee. She is a founding member of the board of directors for the Association for Interdisciplinary Initiatives in Higher Education Law and Policy. Prior to joining Arizona State University in 1989, Tribbensee was an associate with the law firm Evans, Kitchel, and Jenckes. She received her doctorate in counseling psychology from Arizona State University.

Jack Suess is chief information officer at the University of Maryland, Baltimore County (UMBC). Previously, as a systems programmer, he led projects that developed the Unix and network infrastructures and the campus Web development strategy. He was principal investigator for UMBC's very high-speed Backbone Network Service (vBNS) award and has served on multiple NSF and National Institutes of Health panels related to advanced networking. He is an active participant in the Internet2 Middleware Initiative and a member of the EDUCAUSE/Internet2 Computer and Network Security Task Force. Suess is an adjunct professor at UMBC, as well as a presenter at numerous Internet2 and EDUCAUSE conferences on middleware, security, Web technology, and portals.

Daniel A. Updegrove is vice president for Information Technology at the University of Texas at Austin. He is the co-chair of the EDUCAUSE/Internet2 Computer and Network Security Task Force and serves on the higher education advisory committees for Apple Computer and Dell. Updegrove is a consultant, an author, and a frequent speaker on IT strategic planning, networking, computer-based planning models, and computer gaming simulation. Previously he served as director of Information Technology Services at Yale and associate vice provost for Information Systems and Computing at the University of Pennsylvania. Updegrove studied industrial engineering and urban planning at Cornell University.

Gordon D. Wishon is chief information officer at the University of Notre Dame, where he leads all campus technology efforts. Previously he served as associate vice president and associate vice provost for Information Technology at the Georgia Institute of Technology. Wishon spent twenty years in the U.S. Air Force and ended his military career as CIO of the Air Force Institute of Technology. He is the co-chair of the EDUCAUSE/Internet2 Computer and Network Security Task Force. Wishon holds degrees in computer science from West Virginia University and Wright State University in Ohio.

Computer and Network Security in Higher Education

IT Security and Academic Values

Diana Oblinger

The networks and computer systems of colleges and universities abound with student, medical, and financial records; institutional intellectual property for both research and education; and a host of internal and external communications in digital form that are required for normal operations each and every day. Compromised computers on campuses have been used to attack other sites in government and industry. Maintaining a proper level of security for these digital resources is now a critical requirement for the institution.

Although educators may agree with the need for security, differences of opinion arise when specific practices are proposed. For example, technology personnel may consider the use of a firewall a necessary precaution, whereas faculty might see this restriction as an impediment to intellectual freedom. Logging user access is one method of tracking intruders; it also can be considered a threat to privacy. Higher education is faced with the need to apply appropriate security without compromising the fundamental principles of the academy. As a result, it will be important for colleges and universities to determine which principles are most relevant and valued by its particular community. Articulation of a common set of principles may serve as a starting point for campus discussions about computer and network security.

Unique Culture and Environment

Critical aspects of higher education preclude the wholesale adoption of business or government security procedures. The unique mission of higher education and its role in developing individuals is one distinctive feature. Another is an operational environment oftentimes characterized by a transient student population, a residential environment, and the research enterprise. A third is a widely held set of core values that shape the environment and behaviors of the community.

Higher Education's Mission

Three components are used to describe higher education's mission:

- *Education.* Transmitting, transforming, and extending knowledge, as well as promoting the intellectual and moral development of students (Boyer, 1990)

- *Scholarship.* Discovering, integrating, evaluating, and preserving knowledge in all forms (Duderstadt, 2000)

- *Service.* Furnishing special expertise to address the problems and needs of society

As a result, higher education supports a unique combination of activities that include human development and serving as a custodian and conveyor of culture and civilization. These characteristics result in a special social contract between higher education and society. Education clearly provides more than preparation for a career. Education is designed to provide social and cultural understanding for effective citizenship and the development of intellectual capacity that will allow people to continue learning throughout life.

Higher Education Operational Environment

In some respects, higher education replicates a town or small city. There are residential environments, green space to preserve, roads and parking areas to maintain, buildings to operate, and utilities to be provided. This environment creates challenges for computer and network security. For example, students are able to bring their own computer equipment and connect to the network. The software on those computers can be from a host of vendors representing an array of versions, and both students and vendors might be unaware of security problems in those products. The transient nature of the student population and the adoption of wireless capabilities present further challenges.

Although not entirely unique, the instructional and research environments of colleges and universities are more pervasive and open than in government or corporate training departments and research laboratories. Perhaps as an outgrowth of this environment, the academic culture tends to favor experimentation, tolerance, and individual autonomy—all characteristics that make it more difficult to create a culture of computer and network security.

Higher Education Values

Several core academic values are potentially affected by the need for increased computer and network security. These include community, autonomy, privacy, and fairness.

Community

The academic community sees itself not only as a physical place but as a virtual community, as well as a state of mind. Colleges and universities view themselves as a community of scholars, instructors, researchers, students, and staff. The community ideal makes a campus the locus of learning, thoughtful reflection, and intellectual stimulation (Duderstadt, 2000).

This ideal influences the community-based governance of higher education. In shared governance, all relevant parties consult on and participate in decisions (typically faculty and administrators, but often other groups are involved as well). This localized decision-making culture tends to resist attempts by external groups to make its decisions or dictate policy or process.

Although the academic community may seem to be internally focused, the notion of community is very broadly defined in higher education. Most institutions see their mission as serving a much wider community than merely that on campus. As a result, higher education has strong beliefs about inclusiveness, diversity, equitable access, international outreach, and support for the local community. Higher education accepts a responsibility to reach out with its knowledge, expertise, and culture to the external community.

Autonomy

Higher education's strong sense of autonomy may reflect the origins of U.S. higher education, in which institutions were intentionally independent of governmental control. Only in the last half century has public higher education become a dominant force. However, even in public higher education, institutions have adopted mechanisms (for example, governing boards) to maintain independence from government (Eaton, 2000).

That strong sense of autonomy is reflected at the faculty level in values such as academic freedom. Academic freedom embodies the right to pursue controversial topics, ideas, and lines of research without censorship or prior approval. American higher education steadfastly adheres to principles of academic freedom.

A closely related idea, though not synonymous, is that of intellectual freedom. Intellectual freedom provides for free and open scholarly inquiry, freedom of information, and creative expression, including the right to express ideas and receive information in the networked world (Eaton, 2000). One possible interpretation of intellectual freedom is that individuals have the right to open and unfiltered access to the Internet.

Building on its history, higher education holds strongly to values of institutional and faculty autonomy. In such an environment, uniform standards for computer and network security may be difficult to reach.

Privacy

Both U.S. society and higher education place significant value on privacy. Privacy is essential to the exercise of free speech, free thought, and free association. The right to privacy has been upheld based on the Bill of Rights, and many states guarantee privacy in their constitutions and in statute (American Library Association [ALA], 2003). Privacy, in the context of the library, is considered to be "the right to open inquiry without having the subject of one's interest examined or scrutinized by others" (ALA, 2002). Privacy is considered a right of faculty and students.

I Don't Believe So -

Higher education depends on fair information practices, including giving individuals notice regarding how information about them will be used. Higher education also guarantees that information collected will not be shared without permission. Among the implications of privacy is that computer and network users should have the freedom to choose the degree to which personal information is monitored, collected, disclosed, and distributed (ALA, 2002). In the context of libraries, borrowing records are kept confidential. In addition, institutions must ensure the privacy of student records as well as other information, such as patient records, to meet federal requirements.

Fairness

Colleges and universities place great value on fair and predictable treatment of individuals and therefore are invested in defining due process (ALA, 2003).[1] Because fairness and due process are priorities, higher education defines and relies on public policies and procedures that guide institutional behavior, even though they are not always the same as those of the external community. Equal access to information can also be seen as a logical extension of fairness. Equal access implies that users have the same access to information regardless of race, values, gender, culture, ethnic background, or other factors.

It is clear that computer and network security is now essential to protecting privacy and other academic values. It is just as important, however, that measures taken to improve security do not themselves compromise these values.

Principles for Implementing Security in Higher Education

In August 2002, the EDUCAUSE/Internet2 Computer and Network Security Task Force hosted an invitational workshop, sponsored by the National Science Foundation, to establish a set of principles that might guide campus efforts to establish security plans and policies. The goal of the workshop was to ensure that the articulation of higher education's values, particularly those affected by efforts to improve IT security, would guide colleges and universities as they decide how to improve the security of computers and networks.[2] Six principles were identified that may have implications on security policies and procedures.

Civility and Community

Civility and community are critical in higher education. As a result, respect for human dignity, regard for the rights of individuals, and the furtherance of rational discourse must be at the foundation of policies and procedures related to computer and network security. Communities are defined by a set of common values, mutual experiences, shared knowledge, and an ethical framework, as well as a responsibility and commitment to the common good. A tension often exists between standards of civility and the right to freedom of expression.

Colleges and universities should identify reasonable standards of behavior for the use of institutional networks, computers, and related infrastructure as well as acceptable standard security practices and principles to support these core values.

Academic and Intellectual Freedom

Academic freedom is the cornerstone of U.S. higher education. It ensures freedom of inquiry, debate, and communication, which are essential for learning and the pursuit of knowledge. Faculties are entitled to freedom in classroom discussions, research, and the publication of those results, as well as freedom of artistic expression. In addition, individuals are entitled to seek, receive, and impart information, express themselves freely, and access content regardless of the origin, background, or views of those contributing to their creation. Intellectual freedom ensures information access and use, which are essential to a free, democratic society.

Although these principles are widely held among the professoriat, they may not be well understood by other groups, such as technology personnel. As a result, all higher education personnel should be educated to respect academic and intellectual freedom.

Networks and systems must be sufficiently secure to prevent unauthorized modification of online publications and expression, but open enough to enable unfettered online publication and expression. At the same time, colleges and universities, as repositories of information, must determine the degree to which they will provide access to other scholars and citizens, as well as to affiliated students, faculty, and staff.

Privacy and Confidentiality

In the United States, privacy is the right and expectation of all people and an essential element of the academic environment. Confidentiality limits access to certain types of information. Confidentiality and protection of privacy are also required to comply with federal and state law. To the extent possible, the privacy of users should be preserved. Privacy should be protected in information systems, whether personally identifiable information is provided or derived. Fair information practices should guide the collection and disclosure of personal information. Higher education must strike an appropriate balance between confidentiality and use. For example, systems should be designed to enable only authorized access, while keeping the identity of authorized users confidential. These systems should respond to the privacy choices specified by individuals and should be able to implement fair information practices.

Users should have access to information about system logging policies and procedures, including how log data are secured, de-identified or aggregated, and disposed of, as well as information about who has access to the log data, provided that such information does not jeopardize system security. Authentication and authorization systems that ensure compliance with license agreements should not retain individually identifiable user information. In addition, user authentication-authorization logs should be kept separate from system usage logs, with no linking of the two data sets.

Equity, Diversity, and Access

Approaches to security and privacy should respect the equity and diversity goals of higher education by ensuring that access to appropriate information and the Internet is provided equitably to all members of the community. Not everyone interacts with computer or network-based systems with a common set of technical or personal resources. Minority-serving institutions, for example, may be particularly vulnerable to security attacks due to limited resources or a lack of in-house expertise (AN-MSI Security Committee, 2002). Technology should be used to enable all sectors of the community to participate in higher education.

Additional system demands imposed for the purposes of computer and network security should not unreasonably inhibit users whose purposes are legitimate but whose technology resources are limited. In addition, personal disabilities should be accommodated through secure systems. Accommodations for various groups of users should be kept confidential.

Fairness and Process

Access to computer systems, networks, and scholarly resources is essential for individual success within the academy. It is also essential for the delivery of quality services to students, faculty, and staff. Such access should be provided widely to every member of the enterprise. Colleges and universities should develop and communicate explicit policies governing the fair and responsible use of computer and network resources by the academic community. All policies should be accompanied by a description of the process to be followed when any member of the community violates the established policies. Institutions should revoke or limit computer and network access only as a result of a serious offense and after a defined process has been followed.

As a result, campuses should support core higher education values (intellectual freedom, privacy, and civility) and not overreact to individual reports of abuse. Security policies, guidelines, and practices should be discussed and reviewed within the context of each institution's shared governance system. In the event of abuse, campuses must define due process for each member of the community, identifying the appropriate policy and office for guidance in handling incidents (copyright policy, campus posting, noncommercial use, and so forth). Beyond dealing with security breaches, institutions should capitalize on the opportunity a breach represents to reinforce security messages and provide education so that future actions support, rather than undermine, security.

Ethics, Integrity, and Responsibility

Computer and network security is a shared responsibility, relying on the ethics and integrity of the campus community. Respect for confidentiality and privacy is necessary for the vitality of the community. The issue of computer and network security provides a tangible opportunity for teaching and modeling acceptable behavior, as well as reinforcing principles of fair and equitable access to electronic resources.

Inappropriate individual access or use of information infringes on the rights and responsibilities of the entire community. All members of the academic community share a responsibility for security because disruption of services restricts the transmission and exploration of knowledge. Ultimately, security based on integrity and ethics is stronger than security based on technology alone. All members of the academic community must be held to the same ethical standards.

Selected Security Practices

A wide range of practices can be used to improve computer and network security. Some of these practices have the potential to raise concerns about their appropriateness for an academic setting. Colleges and universities face the challenge of balancing the need for security and the techniques available with their institutions' values, and of discussing the relationships and tradeoffs with a degree of precision that can lead to acceptable, positive results.

- *Authentication.* The use of a user ID and password is among the most straightforward of security approaches. However, password-guessing software (available on the Web) makes many passwords vulnerable. Can or should institutions enforce strict adherence to procedures, such as changing passwords on a regular basis or using complex passwords that include symbols, alpha, and numeric characters? If so, does this compromise autonomy?
- *Firewalls.* Many organizations use firewalls to limit access to networks from the public Internet. A firewall prevents outsiders from accessing internal or private resources. Does this technique pose an unacceptable limitation on access to higher education?
- *Packet filtering by source.* Packet filtering provides a passive means of security by allowing only packets that come from recognized sources or networks to enter the network. Does such a practice unnecessarily restrict access?

- *Virtual private network.* A virtual private network (VPN) establishes a secure "tunnel" between the user and the server. VPNs protect networks from unauthorized access and log user actions. Does the creation of a VPN unfairly restrict access to higher education's resources?

- *E-mail content filtering.* E-mail can transmit sensitive information (such as patient or student information) and viruses. Institutions can install software filters to screen content, preventing intentional or accidental transmission of sensitive information. Does content filtering represent an invasion of privacy? Does it threaten intellectual freedom?

- *Web content filtering.* Web content filtering programs allow organizations to track Web-based activities, such as students downloading music or video over the residence hall network. They can also detect the downloading of malicious code (often done by unsuspecting users). Are such programs a violation of privacy? Do they challenge intellectual freedom?

- *Logging.* A common security practice is the creation of logs or records. Logs can include time/date stamps, time online, sites accessed, and so on. Is such logging an invasion of privacy?

- *Sniffers.* Sniffer programs monitor and analyze network data with the goal of identifying problems. Sniffer programs can also capture network traffic and read data in packets, as well as the source and destination addresses. Sniffers can be used legitimately (to identify network problems) or illegitimately (to intercept messages) (Whatis, 2000). Could these programs stifle intellectual freedom?

- *Scanning.* It is possible to scan computers on a network to ensure that the machines have no viruses or vulnerabilities. Is scanning a computer without the users' consent an invasion of privacy?

- *Intrusion detection.* Intrusion detection is based on finding atypical patterns in data and network traffic, which may be a sign of intrusion (for example, someone making repeated attempts to log in using random passwords). Intrusion detection systems use network logs; those who monitor the logs can deal with an attack by shutting off access or by "identifying a hacker's dorm room and calling campus security" ("Security," 2003). Is this an invasion of privacy? Does it hamper intellectual freedom?

• *Biometrics*. Biometrics is a security technique that uses physical traits (fingerprints, iris scans) as added security beyond user names and passwords or access cards. Some emerging systems target behavioral traits, such as how a person walks. Does biometrics invade individuals' privacy?

These and other questions may arise as a campus implements or strengthens its security plan. It is best that they be addressed in an open dialogue that recognizes the need for a proper level of security to protect academic values.

Conclusion

Colleges and universities face a growing number of security challenges. Institutions may begin to address these with well-defined security policies that have been clearly communicated to faculty, staff, administrators, and students. Policy alone will not suffice, though. Procedures and educational programs will be needed to ensure that security is as strong as is needed in relation to the risks. Changing the behavior of a large, diverse community can be daunting. Even more difficult is creating a culture in which everyone on campus considers security a part of normal, day-to-day activities. How do we find the "right" level of security, one that balances ease and openness of access with protection from those who might cause harm to the institution?

Computer and network security is absolutely necessary but must be implemented with sensitivity to higher education's unique environment. Discussion among the academic, technology, and security communities will allow higher education to find the appropriate balance between traditional values and principles and current needs for computer and network security.

Notes

1. Due process is not intended as a legal term in this context.

2. On August 27, 2002, Columbia University hosted an invitational workshop to establish a set of overarching principles that should guide any campus effort to establish security plans or policies. The goal of the workshop was to ensure that the articulation of higher education's values, particularly those affected by efforts to improve IT security, would guide colleges and universities as they decide how to improve the security of computers and networks. Based on research into principles articulated by a variety of academic groups, such as the American Association of University Professors, Association of Research Libraries, and Center for Academic Integrity, and on statements by invited experts, the group proposed a set of six principles that higher education can use to steer its efforts to improve computer and network security. This was one of a series of workshops organized by the EDUCAUSE/Internet2 Computer and Network Security Task Force and supported by a grant from the National Science Foundation.

References

American Library Association. *Privacy: An Interpretation of the Library Bill of Rights*. [www.ala.org/alaorg/oif/privacyinterpretation.pdf]. 2002.

American Library Association. *Principles for the Networked World*. [www.ala.org/oitp/principles/pdf]. 2003.

AN-MSI (Advanced Networking with Minority-Serving Institutions) Security Committee. "Developing Network Security at Minority-Serving Institutions: Building Upon the Title V Collaborative Effort Model." Unpublished manuscript, 2002.

Boyer, E. L. *Scholarship Reconsidered: Priorities of the Professoriate*. San Francisco: Jossey-Bass, 1990, p. 24.

Duderstadt, J. J. *A University for the 21st Century*. Ann Arbor: The University of Michigan Press, 2000, p. 14.

Eaton, J. "Core Academic Values, Quality, and Regional Accreditation: The Challenge of Distance Learning." [www.chea.org/Commentary/core-values.cfm#values]. 2000.

"Security." [www.cio.com/summaries/web/security/index.html]. Jan. 2003.

Whatis. [whatis.techtarget.com/definition/0,,sid9_gci213016,00.html]. 2002.

2

Organizing for Improved Security

Jeff Recor

Imagine you just started a new job as a newspaper carrier. You are not familiar with the route, the customers, or the rigors of the job. As you receive your allotment of papers on your first day, your boss says to you, "Make sure these papers are all delivered every morning by 10:00 A.M. no matter how bad the weather gets or how sick you become." With little experience delivering papers and even less information about your customers, you take off to deliver your papers and find your way as you go. You have faith in your abilities and trust that you can work out any problems as they arise.

This allegory depicts the way many IT departments within academia have treated information security. Information security has typically been something to be added later. Worse yet, it is an area that has languished within information technology departments for years as the responsibility of overburdened system administrators or general IT staffers.

In the private sector, organizing for improved security typically is associated with establishing a formal information protection program (IPP). Steps that are taken by private sector organizations to establish a formal IPP include the following:

- Develop a single point of leadership responsible for the security function.

- Develop a support organization that is focused solely on security functions.

- Develop a security plan of action.

- Obtain operational, political, and financial support for the implementation of the plan of action.

Due to the open nature of academic environments and the protection of freedoms for the pursuit of knowledge, many higher learning institutions do not conform to the same practices that the private sector utilizes to organize for security. Fortunately, more and more academic institutions are recognizing the inherent risks associated with increased reliance on the use of information technology. As stated in the *National Strategy to Secure Cyberspace*, institutions of higher learning are starting to recognize the need to protect their resources and are examining ways to implement security functions that enable them to support their operations efficiently and affordably (*National Strategy*, 2003, pp. 40–41).

Formalizing a security-focused function within an academic environment is challenging because of the need to balance *convenience* (free and easy access to information) and *openness* (the ability to exchange ideas and information in a free and open environment) with *security* (the freedom from risk or danger). However, recent legislative, legal, competitive, and student pressures have forced academic institutions to rethink their approaches to handling information security. Colleges and universities are developing new security-focused roles and organizations within IT and other departments to support the mission of the institution. The old tactic of scaring people to act through fear, uncertainty, and doubt is being replaced with arguments supporting improved security and individual empowerment that does not compromise freedom of expression.

Establishment of a Security Infrastructure

All academic institutions can benefit from establishing an organized security infrastructure. This infrastructure comprises people, processes, and technology that can be directed toward securing the institutions' assets within an open campus environment. It is no longer acceptable to put policies and procedures in place without some type of security hierarchy to support them.

The security support function can be dispersed among the many different departments on campus, or it can be centralized under a single entity such as information technology. Several factors can influence the way in which the security function is organized within an academic institution, such as

- Support of executive-level management and trustees

- Support of internal staff

- Requirements of external business partnerships (hospitals, military, private sector, and so forth)

- Politics within the institution

- Size of the institution

- Leadership and cooperation of IT and financial management teams

Each of these items can have a direct impact on the applicability of a formalized information security function.

Regardless of the method used to organize for improved security, institutions need to take action to protect their systems, people, and processes. Each year more security incidents occur that could have been prevented if the institution had taken action and properly incorporated information security functions into its day-to-day operations. Examples include the incident of a University of Delaware student who was able to successfully hijack the passwords of several professors and change her grades (Read, 2002), and the incidents that caused federal officials to issue an alert regarding the security of college networks (Foster, 2002).

Institutions need to focus on the following critical functions when organizing to improve security:

- Developing a security plan of action that can be shared

- Obtaining support for the implementation of the plan of action

- Developing a mechanism for measuring progress of the security function

- Formulating partnerships and alliances to enhance internal capabilities

- Establishing security leadership

- Hiring or developing security expertise on staff

Developing a Security Plan of Action

The first step to organizing for improved security is to establish a security plan. The security plan will help the organization design its security strategy for supporting the operations of the institution. It will also formally define the items that need to be protected, the value they hold to the institution, the leadership structure needed to proactively manage the process, and many other operational details that will provide protection for the campus environment. The security plan will act as the overall security process blueprint, much as the security policies and procedures guide employee behaviors.

Obtaining Support for the Plan

Support from all levels of the institution is critical to a successful implementation. In general it is easier to obtain support for the plan if its constructs have been developed and can be discussed among senior management. Communication of the plan, its reason for being, and its potential costs and benefits need to be clearly and concisely articulated to upper management in order to gain support.

The idea that information security is someone else's problem is quickly disappearing. According to Michael McRobbie, vice president for information technology at Indiana University, "Colleges have a well-deserved reputation for lax network security. As a result, they risk increased insurance costs and expensive lawsuits" (Olsen, 2002, p. A35). However, in this environment of increased risk, many organizations still do not believe they need to worry about information security. So how do you sell upper management on the fact that they need to take information security seriously?

1. *Show them that information security adds value to the institution.* Although securing a campus environment takes time and money, it is a task that ultimately will protect staff, students, and partners, while also mitigating exposure to lawsuits, intellectual property loss, and employee problems.

2. *Match security needs to operational functions.* Gaining upper management support will take more than explaining the bits and bytes of the technology involved in protecting the institution. Strategy needs to be put into plain English and designed to support the goals of the institution.

3. *Establish frequent and concise reporting mechanisms to show improvement based on your actions.* For many managers, not hearing that anything bad has happened lulls them into a false sense of security. Often when security mechanisms are working properly, nothing will happen. Make sure management understands that no news is good news—especially if you can communicate that message regularly.

4. *Include security issues early in budgeting and IT planning processes.* Too often security technology is added "after the fact" and is

not integrated into a project from the beginning. By getting involved early, management may see the value that planning for security can have across the entire spectrum of project management.

The plan will also need the support of the department heads within the institution, as well as internal IT staff. To achieve this level of cooperation, academic institutions will sometimes establish committees consisting of representatives from different departments and use them as a "sounding board" for tweaking the plan's goals and objectives.

Measuring Progress

Part of the process of organizing for improved security is to be able to learn from mistakes. Establishing a feedback loop through regular surveys will assist all personnel associated with the security function to learn how to better support the changing security environment. By monitoring numbers and types of security incidents, IT staff can track trends and develop more effective incident response strategies.

It is also important to monitor community satisfaction and awareness. Are faculty, students, and department staff pleased with the support they receive from the security program? Are there improvements that could be made? Asking these types of questions will enable communication to flow back and forth between the personnel performing security functions and their constituents.

Forming Partnerships and Alliances

Many different types of programs are being developed to help form bridges between private and public sector organizations. One commonly seen partnership of this type involves outsourcing central IT support. This has been done successfully at many institutions, with the goal of having better end-user support, lower costs, and improved service delivery.

Outsourcing the security function to a third party is a viable option for institutions that do not have the ability to handle security events internally. Of course there are pros and cons for such an arrangement, as with any outsourcing relationship. The benefits to the institution of outsourcing security include gaining the experience of security "experts," having flexibility in meeting budget constraints, and obtaining a reduction in costs associated with maintaining the security function in-house. Among the downsides of such a relationship, the institution does not develop any in-house expertise and there is the potential for costs to increase. It is important to note that in any case, the responsibility and accountability for securing campus systems still rest with information technology leadership.

A new era of partnership is developing among employers, IT vendors, training organizations, and the public sector, fueled in many cases by the shortage of capable security professionals in today's workforce. Institutions are considering all types of ways to leverage the private sector to increase its internal security expertise, as well as its capability to deliver educational services securely. Several institutions use their security teams as internal consultants who will charge for time according to use of their services. Still other institutions have been crafting agreements with companies such as Cisco, Microsoft, Hewlett-Packard, and Symantec to exchange security expertise and information on a contractual basis (www.cerias.purdue.edu/news_and_events/news/view_story.php?id= 75). All of these types of arrangements help ensure that the institution's security program accomplishes its goals and stays current with the latest trends.

Establishing Security Leadership

Critical to organizing for improved security is establishing dedicated leadership and skill sets. During the previous year, one of the most popular topics for discussion at security conferences and workshops involved the establishment of a security leadership role and skills to support the function. Ideally, a dedicated security team would be led by an experienced professional who would provide expertise for developing and recommending policies and procedures, assessing vulnerabilities, detecting intrusions, responding to incidents, and developing an awareness program. However, many college and university environments do not support the creation of a single leadership position responsible for information security functions.

Many private-sector organizations are starting to support the addition of a new executive-level title called the chief security officer (CSO). Management consulting firm Booz Allen Hamilton in January 2002 surveyed firms with more than $1 billion dollars in annual revenues and found that 54 percent of the seventy-two chief executive officers it surveyed have a chief security officer in place. Ninety percent have been in that position for more than two years. When there is no chief security officer in place, chief information officers are more likely than other executives to have security responsibilities, the survey found (http://cin.earthweb.com/news/article.php/10493_997701). This position is similar to that of the chief information officer but is limited in scope to information security responsibilities.

Because security cuts across every line of business and every strategic decision, more and more companies are adding this position to their executive team. Typically, the CSO will report to a senior functional executive, such as a chief operating officer, chief administration officer, or head of legal counsel, and will coordinate security efforts across organizational units, including information technology, human resources, communications, legal, and facilities management.

Although this type of executive-level position is starting to gain momentum in the private sector, it does not appear to be catching on with colleges and universities. One of the main issues with establishing a leadership role for the information security responsibility is where this position obtains its executive-level support. Many CSOs currently report to the chief information officer and have to learn how to navigate through the IT political landscape in order to support other business units. Several very large organizations have recently started to move the reporting structure of the CSO to the chief executive officer. Within academic environments, appointing a single person with security leadership responsibilities can be a difficult task because of cultural, political, and organizational challenges. The size of the institution can also provide unique challenges to organizing security functions through a centralized leadership role. In the private sector, the role of chief security officer is often a shared function with the police office or public safety team.

Hiring and Developing Security Expertise

Providing leadership for information security functions is an important undertaking. In addition to choosing a leader for the security function, a team of individuals should also be considered to support the function. Several recent studies have shown security staffing levels to be erratic and unorganized. As a typical example of the proportion of security staff to information technology staff, a recent study by Computer Economics ranks IT security staffing levels by size of company (see Table 2.1). Another staffing survey, performed by *Information Security* magazine, shows the same type of information relating to the size of security teams (see Figure 2.1).

One of the items that these types of surveys highlight is the challenge that organizations face when trying to find staff with dedicated security skill sets. Because creating dedicated security teams is a relatively new endeavor for dealing effectively with security challenges, further studies need to be done to show how companies are handling security staffing issues.

Basic Security Functions

Another way to view security staffing is through the analysis of roles and responsibilities. A basic set of security functions should be established regardless of the size of the institution. Every institution

Table 2.1. IT Security Staffing Levels.

Number of Employees	Number of Security Staff				
	Zero	1 to 2	3 to 5	6 to 10	More than 10
	Percentage of Organizations				
Less than 25	13.8	48.2	24.1	3.4	10.3
26 to 50	9.1	81.9	0.0	9.1	0.0
51 to 100	0.0	56.2	25.0	0.0	18.8
101 to 250	14.3	42.8	21.4	14.3	7.1
251 to 500	0.0	26.7	46.7	6.7	20.0
501 to 1,000	15.4	46.2	23.1	0.0	15.4
1,001 to 2,000	7.1	7.1	35.7	28.6	21.4
2,001 to 5,000	12.5	6.2	18.8	18.8	43.7
5,001 to 10,000	0.0	7.1	42.9	21.4	28.6
Over 10,000	0.0	5.8	14.7	8.8	70.6
All organizations	7.0	29.6	24.4	10.5	28.5

Source: "IT Security: Perceptions, Awareness and Practice." *Computer Economics*, Aug. 2002, 4. Reprinted with permission of Computer Economics, Inc. (www.computereconomics.com).

that utilizes computer technology has common functions that require some level of security functionality to protect information assets. These functions can be separated into three distinct areas: physical security, business operations security, and business continuity.

Physical Security

Physical security responsibilities can include locking up sensitive resources and information, monitoring the facilities, and using guards and alarms. For most institutions, these physical security tasks are designed and managed by a group that is separate from the IT organization. With the advent of new software and hardware that can join digital and physical monitoring, the management of physical security can be rolled into the traditional IT hierarchy or

Figure 2.1. Number of In-House Security Staff.

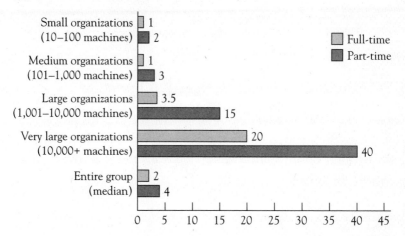

Source: Andrew Briney and Frank Prince, "Does Size Matter? The Size of Your Organization May Be the Single Biggest Barometer of IT Security's Effectiveness." *Information Security,* Sept. 2002, p. 45 [www.inforsecuritymag.com/2002/sep/ 2002survey.pdf]. Reprinted with permission.

campus police function. The new industry buzzword for software vendors addressing this market need is *security convergence*.

Operational Security

Operational security functions include all of the traditional security responsibilities, such as placing firewalls to protect connections to the Internet, using access control management techniques, and auditing access controls and internal processes. Traditional security skills have been built around this core set of functionality, which includes firewall, intrusion detection, antivirus, and other product integration skill sets.

Business Continuity

The final category of common security functions is business continuity. Business continuity responsibilities include activities that provide the institution with the ability to continue operations in the event of a disaster or other catastrophic event. Other activities that may fall into this category include data backup, load balancing, disaster recovery, and performance monitoring.

Security Professionals Assigned to Function

Based on these common functions, many institutions hire staff to manage day-to-day operations based on their needs in these three areas. Some of the more common job titles and their responsibilities are discussed next.

Security Administrator

The security administrator provides all technical administrative support for the IT organization, including performing liaison functions for other departments that may need support. The security administrator is responsible for maintaining security technology and reviewing log files for malicious activity.

Security Analyst

The security analyst assists the IT and information security staff with ensuring that all applicable business and policy requirements are met with the correct control functions and processes. The security analyst is often charged with reviewing the applicability of new technology and processes to see whether the organization can benefit from their use. In some instances, the security analyst may work with auditors or outside consulting organizations to perform risk assessments and review business continuity.

Security Engineer

The security engineer is a consultant in technical systems management who is the focal point and leader for design and implementation of security technology that supports the business objectives of the organization. People in this position work with various departments to ensure that the information security technology is designed, installed, and maintained to function correctly.

Certification of Security Professionals

When hiring dedicated security personnel, most institutions are concerned about both skills and salary. As market demand has increased, professionals with security expertise have been in short supply, and salaries have risen. Individuals with industry certifications are of particular interest; they bring defined sets of skills and experience to the table, and consequently may expect higher compensation. Certifications can cover everything from learning a common body of knowledge to focusing on a specific technology. Although professional certifications do not guarantee a successful hire or good organizational fit, they do provide the hiring institution with some assurance that the individual has basic competence in the topics covered by the program. Some of the more popular certifications include the following:

- *Certified information systems security professional (CISSP)*. Created and maintained by the International Information Systems Security Certification Consortium, the CISSP requires four years of security-related experience plus the passing of a six-hour exam. Candidates are expected to master a common body of knowledge and adhere to professional ethics while certified (www.isc2.org).
- *Global information assurance certification (GIAC)*. The SANS (System Administration, Audit, Network, Security) Institute rolled out the GIAC in 1999 to address the need for specific technology mastery. The GIAC framework provides assurances that the candidates have mastered specific areas of technology, such as firewalls, intrusion detection, and incident handling (www.sans.org).
- *Security +*. The Computing Technology Industry Association (CompTIA) has developed an international benchmark certification

for security practitioners that measures foundational knowledge. This certification is considered to be a starting point for practitioners starting out in the field (www.comptia.org).

Certification Magazine recently published a survey of the top security-related certifications as well as expected salary ranges of professionals with these certifications (www.certmag.com/articles/templates/cmag_sg.asp?articleid=71&zoneid=74.) The bottom line is that most surveys show that personnel with security certifications command salaries anywhere between $50,000 and $100,000 in the marketplace today.

Use of Consultants

An alternative to hiring dedicated security staff is to engage the services of an outside consulting organization. Institutions may use the services of an outside firm from time to time as a "check and balance" to measuring internal progress and effectiveness. Although outside security experts can help augment staff roles, hiring them is an expensive way to handle security functions day to day. Computer Economics, as part of the study referenced earlier, also took a look at the practices of organizations hiring outside consultants, as reflected in Table 2.2. This table shows that the institutions that use consultants the most are those that have a heavy emphasis on issues of legal or regulatory compliance.

Conclusion

The campus environment is constantly changing. Information security is a process that is also dynamic and becoming more important in the day-to-day operations of the institution. Just like the experienced newspaper carrier mentioned at the beginning of the chapter, once the route is defined the job is simply nothing more than focusing on delivering the papers. By organizing to improve security, institutions can improve their security posture and help protect our nation's critical infrastructure.

Table 2.2. Organizations Contracting with a Security Consulting Firm During 2002.

Industry Sector	Percentage of Total Respondents	Percentage of Respondents Who Have Contracted with a Security Consulting Firm During 2002
Banking, finance and insurance	14.6	27.9
Education	6.6	4.9
Government	16.5	21.3
Health care	4.7	8.2
Manufacturing	11.3	13.2
Professional services	33.5	14.8
Retail, wholesale distribution	6.1	8.2
Trade services	2.8	1.6
Transportation and utilities	3.8	0.0
Number of Employees		
Less than 25	17.9	9.8
26 to 50	5.2	4.9
51 to 100	9.0	3.3
101 to 250	8.5	3.3
251 to 500	7.5	6.6
501 to 1,000	6.6	9.8
1,001 to 2,000	7.5	8.2
2,001 to 5,000	9.9	9.8
5,001 to 10,000	8.0	13.1
Over 10,000	19.8	31.1
Annual Revenue		
Under $1,000,000	22.3	20.0
$1,000,001 to $5,000,000	10.2	9.1
$5,000,001 to $10,000,000	6.6	7.3
$10,000,001 to $20,000,000	11.7	7.3
$20,000,001 to $50,000,000	8.1	3.6
$50,000,001 to $100,000,000	9.1	5.5
$100,000,001 to $1 billion	10.7	14.5
Over $1 billion	21.3	32.7

Source: "IT Security: Perceptions, Awareness and Practice." *Computer Economics,* Aug. 2002, 4. Reprinted with permission of Computer Economics, Inc. (www.computereconomics.com).

References

Foster, A. "Federal Officials Issue Alert on Security of College Networks."
    Chronicle of Higher Education, July 5, 2002, A32.

National Strategy to Secure Cyberspace. [www.securecyberspace.gov]. 2003.

Olsen, F. "The Growing Vulnerability of Campus Networks." *Chronicle of Higher
    Education*, Mar. 15, 2002, A35.

Read, B. "Delaware Student Allegedly Changed Her Grades Online." *Chronicle
    of Higher Education*, August 2, 2002, A29.

3

Conducting a Risk Analysis

Randy Marchany

A common response to computer security professionals' efforts to secure enterprise and desktop systems is "I don't have anything on my computer that a hacker would want." This statement is true most of the time. Most hackers really don't want your data; rather, they want your computer. They want to use your system to attack other sites. The distributed denial-of-service (DDOS) attacks of the past years are an example of this strategy. Hackers often compromise systems not to steal the data that reside on them but to use the systems to attack other systems. An early DDOS attack involved close to 300 systems used to attack a single site. It's interesting to note that the hackers had complete access to any file on these systems and they could have modified or deleted any files, yet they didn't. How do the hackers get in despite efforts to keep them out?

In 1998, the Internet Audit Project (Siri, 1998) scanned more than 36 million Internet hosts for common and publicized security vulnerabilities. The scan exposed large numbers of vulnerabilities (more than 700,000) to the most common security threats. "These open points of penetration immediately threaten the security of their affiliated networks, putting many millions of systems in commercial, academic, government and military organizations at a high compromise risk" (Siri, 1998, unnumbered). Every vulnerability discovered by the scan could have been eliminated by proper application of *patches*, or updates to the software that are typically supplied by the vendor. This little test, which took only twenty-one days to run and tested for only eighteen vulnerabilities, showed just how easy it would be to compromise systems in critical industries and the devastating effect that these compromises could have. Ensuring that a university's assets are not vulnerable becomes the primary role of the institution's security officer, system administrators, and internal audit group. Cooperation among the three groups is essential.

Risk Analysis

A critical activity for the security officer, auditor, and IT department to undertake is an *institutional risk analysis*. Conducting a risk analysis is a process of identifying assets, the risks to those assets, and procedures to mitigate the risks to the assets. Individual users and their institutions need to understand what risks exist in their information asset environment and how those risks can be reduced or even eliminated. Embarking on a process to complete such an analysis or self-assessment is critical in today's advanced technological world. The process is one that will benefit both the individual department and the institution as a whole. When conducted in partnership by IT and institutional auditors, a risk analysis can not only provide valuable information to the university but also will carry the weight of a united perspective when it comes time to make decisions about acceptable levels of risk and to secure funding and implement the plan for mitigating risks.

Many good models are available that detail how to perform a risk management study, including how to classify information technology assets and risks. These models provide a foundation for doing more than just avoiding risk—they all provide recommended approaches for identifying weaknesses in the systems, processes for making decisions about how to protect assets, and ways to help evaluate and answer the question, How much security is enough?

Selected Models

The National Infrastructure Protection Center (NIPC) released a document entitled "Risk Management: An Essential Guide to Protecting Critical Assets" in November 2002. This document discusses a five-step risk assessment model: (1) asset assessment, (2) threat assessment, (3) vulnerability assessment, (4) risk assessment, and (5) identification of countermeasure options. The guide includes some examples in tabular format of each of the assessment phases. These examples are useful in helping an organization perform a risk management study. The model is discussed in detail in "The Risk Assessment: Five Steps to Better Risk Management Decisions" (Jopeck, 1997).

Mohammad H. Qayoumi (2002) wrote an excellent guide on continuity planning titled *Mission Continuity Planning: Strategically Assessing and Planning for Threats to Operations*. This booklet was published by the National Association of College and Business Officers (NACUBO) and contains excellent information on risk management, disaster preparedness, business continuity planning, calculating system reliability, and addressing facilities-related risks.

NACUBO also released a document called "Developing a Strategy to Manage Enterprisewide Risk in Higher Education" (Cassidy and others, 2001). This publication presents a definition of risk, the drivers of risk, advice on implementing a risk management plan, and how to advance the risk management agenda to management.

The National Institute of Science and Technology (NIST) published *Security Self-Assessment Guide for Information Technology Systems* (Swanson, 2001). The guide contains a questionnaire template that can be adapted to your site's needs. The guide is most useful for federal government agencies, since it uses NIST's federal IT security assessment framework, which standardizes five levels of security criteria.

Case Study: The Star Project

In the late 1990s, a newspaper article about a cyberattack on a university in Virginia prompted a member of the Virginia Tech Board of

Visitors to ask whether a similar attack could happen at Virginia Tech. How vulnerable were Virginia Tech's networks and systems to outside intrusion? This question led to a directive to form a committee to investigate and report on the status of the IT organization's assets. This became known as the STAR (Security Targeting and Analysis of Risks) process (security.vt.edu/playitsafe/index.phtml).

The Information Security Committee was made up of department managers and system and network administrators. This blend of management and technical people was critical in balancing the contrasting viewpoints of security versus access. The prejudices and perspectives of the members resulted in a healthy exchange of viewpoints.

The committee was charged with identifying and prioritizing information systems assets, associating risks with those assets, and listing controls that could be applied to mitigate the risks. Although the committee did not initially consider assets outside of the IT organization, in later iterations of the process departmental assets were evaluated.

Identifying Assets

The committee first compiled a list of division assets and categorized them as critical, essential, or normal assets. An asset was deemed *critical* if the loss of its function would result in the university ceasing to function as a business entity. An *essential* asset would cripple the university's capacity to function, but it could survive for a week or so without the asset. All effort would be made to restore the function within a week. An asset was deemed *normal* if its loss resulted in some inconvenience. The interesting result of this process was that no one wanted to classify his or her asset as normal. The committee avoided trying to classify which components of the network were critical, such as the routers, cable plant, hubs, and switches, by treating the entire network as a critical asset. (These individual network components would have been considered if this had been an audit of the network group.) A sample asset list and classifications are shown in Table 3.1.

Table 3.1. Sample Classification System for Assets and Their Priority.

Description of Asset	Machine Name	Priority[a]
Authentication-authorization services	host1.dept.edu	C
DNS name server	host2.dept.edu	C
Physical plant, environmental servers	host3.dept.edu	C
DNS name server (secondary)	host4.dept.edu	C
Network (routers, servers, modems, etc.)	host5.dept.edu	C
HR database server	host6.dept.edu	E
Payroll server	host7.dept.edu	E
Production control servers	host8.dept.edu	N
Client systems (Win95/NT, Macs)	host9.dept.edu	N
Database group "crash-and-burn" system	host10.dept.edu	N

[a]C, critical element; E, essential; N, normal.

Once a list of assets had been determined and categorized, the committee prioritized them by criticality to the division's operation. This was done by committee vote. Table 3.2 illustrates a weight matrix that was used to record votes for the assets. The committee votes are recorded in the individual cells, and the total votes for the asset are recorded in the bottom row. The example in Table 3.2 shows that the top three critical assets are the network, the physical plant and environmental servers, and the primary DNS server. Assets were prioritized by voting whether asset 1 was more critical than asset 2, and so forth.

Determining Risk

The committee followed a similar procedure for listing and categorizing the risks to the assets. Four criteria were used in determining a critical risk: (1) It would be extremely expensive to fix, (2) it would result in the loss of a critical service, (3) it would result in heavy, negative publicity, especially outside the organization, and (4) it had a high probability of occurring. Table 3.3 shows the critical risks as determined by the committee. A voting procedure similar to that used to prioritize the assets was used by the committee to prioritize

Table 3.2. Sample Asset Weight Matrix to Prioritize IT Assets.

	A/A	DNS(p)	Plant	DNS(s)	Network	HR
Authentication-authorization services		9	9	4.5	9	5
DNS name server (primary)	0		9	0	9	5
Physical plant, environmental servers	0	0		2	9	4.5
DNS name server (secondary)	3.5	9	7		9	5
Network (routers, servers, modems, etc.)	0	0	0	0		0
HR database server	4	4	3.5	4	9	
TOTAL VOTES	7.5	22	28.5	10.5	45	19.5

the risks. The end result of this entire process was an asset matrix listing every IT asset, an asset weight matrix rank ordering the criticality of the asset, a risk matrix listing every risk, and a risk weight matrix for the set of risks associated with the asset.

Once a final list of assets and risks was developed, the team members mapped the rank-ordered assets and risks into a single matrix. This risk-asset matrix provided guidance as to the order in which each asset and risk were to be examined.

Finally, the STAR team created a controls matrix that listed all of the possible controls that would mitigate the risks listed in the risk matrix. The team did not prioritize these controls; instead it created another risk-asset-controls matrix that listed the possible controls for a particular risk to a particular asset.

Table 3.3. Sample Risk Classification Listing Critical Risks Only.

Risk	Description
Clear text	Clear text data moving among our systems and networks
Client system access control	Control of access to distributed desktop client workstations
Construction mistakes	Service interruptions during construction, renovations
Key person dependency	Too few staff to cover critical responsibilities
Natural disaster	Flood, earthquake, fire, etc.
Passwords	Selection, security, number of passwords, etc.
Physical security (IS internal)	IS private space (machine room, wire closets, offices, etc.)
Physical security (IS external)	IS public space (laboratories, classrooms, library, etc.)
Spoofing	E-mail and IP address forgery or circumvention
Data disclosure	Inappropriate acquisition or release of university data
System administration practices	Adequacy of knowledge, skills, and procedures
Operational policies	Appropriate strategies, directions, and policies

Applying Controls

Risk and asset matrices formed a blueprint for applying controls to the assets. The STAR team developed a set of compliance matrices that corresponds with the risks and assets listed earlier. This set of compliance matrices contains detailed line-item actions to verify that a particular task has been performed. A color-coding system is used to denote success or failure of a particular line item. This provides an auditor, security manager, or system administrator with a quick way to verify the compliance of an asset with the risk analysis process.

Figure 3.1 shows a portion of the original overall compliance matrix, which is similar to the executive summary portion of an audit. It lists an overall rating for each critical asset. The risks are listed along the y-axis and the assets are listed along the x-axis. There is a corresponding set of matrices associated with each risk line item that contains more detailed information on the tests required to determine the vulnerability of an asset to the particular

Figure 3.1. Summary Compliance Matrix Showing the Overall State of an Asset in Relation to Identified Risks.

	IS ASSETS			
	Site 1	Site 2	Site 3	Site 4
OVERALL	OK			
System admin. practices	OK	OK		
Data disclosure	**FAIL**	OK	CAUTION	
Passwords	OK	CAUTION	OK	
Key person dependency	OK	**FAIL**	FUTURE	FUTURE
Physical security	CAUTION	CAUTION	OK	FUTURE

UNIX security risks

risk. A set of detailed commands needed to check the system is at the lowest level. The test procedure is as follows:

1. Use the detailed command list to perform the test.

2. Record the results in the detailed compliance matrix.

3. Compute an overall score for an asset (70 percent "OK" means an "OK" score at this level, for example) and record the score in the overall compliance matrix.

The matrices allow Virginia Tech staff to track progress in addressing the risks over the long term. They provide a foundation on which to apply the scarce resources to perform a cost-benefit analysis of the assets and risks.

After conducting analyses with the IT organization, the STAR team took the matrices and the process and made them available to every department in the university. STAR provided the common risks set to departments and encouraged each to add its own risks. The end result is that each department can now look at the risks it has in common with others and at its own unique risks about which it needs to be concerned.

STAR Today

The STAR methodology is still in use at Virginia Tech today, and it continues to be refined, even after seven years. It took the committee about one year of meeting once every two weeks to develop and refine the methodology. Subsequent risk analysis projects are much less time consuming, since the basic matrices now exist. In 2002 the STAR team completed the seventh iteration of the risk analysis process in one month. Support from university leadership has also been critical. Securing the approval of the top management at Virginia Tech ensured a 98 percent on-time return rate of the individual departmental risk analysis reports. This simply confirms what every security office has known: management buy-in of the process is critical to its success.

Although STAR's main purpose is to provide a repeatable method for prioritizing assets and risks to those assets, one of the major modifications to the process during the last few years revolves around asset classification. Initially, computer systems or the network were identified as assets, but the team is now moving toward identifying business processes as assets. This, in turn, creates a layered approach to asset classification. For example, at the top level, student registration is identified as a business process and asset. It comprises (1) departments that manage the business process, that is, the registrar; (2) the software management group that manages the software that runs the student registration process, for example, SCT's Banner software; (3) the information systems group that manages the machines that run the Banner software; and finally, (4) the actual machines that run the Banner software. The STAR methodology can then be used to prioritize assets at any level of this tree. Virginia Tech is now using this layered approach to help identify key business processes, thereby in turn helping design a better disaster recovery procedure. An additional benefit to "layering" the assets is being able to see the dependencies that a particular asset needs to accomplish its mission.

The checklists used to measure compliance have also changed, and Virginia Tech has adapted the STAR methodology to use the Center for Internet Security's (CIS) (www.cissecurity.com) security benchmarks (replacing the colored matrices) to measure how a computer system complies with local security requirements. The CIS benchmarks are free and prove to be an excellent resource for various UNIX, Windows, and router platforms. The CIS benchmarks provide a straightforward method of configuring a system according to the STAR analysis. CIS benchmarks are applied to the critical assets. The CIS toolkit provides a scanning tool that rates the asset based on the benchmark. This score presents a target value for auditors.

Figure 3.2 shows the output screen of the CIS Windows 2000 scanning tool. When the necessary services are enabled on a critical asset, the scanning tool reports a score for each service. This scoring method provides an auditor with a simple way of checking an asset for compliance. If the asset scores a 7.3 or higher, then its local policies have been set in compliance with the risk analysis. A lower score requires justification from the asset system administrators or owners. It does not mean the system is less secure; instead, it generally means that something required the system security policies to

Figure 3.2. Sample CIS Scanning Tool Output.

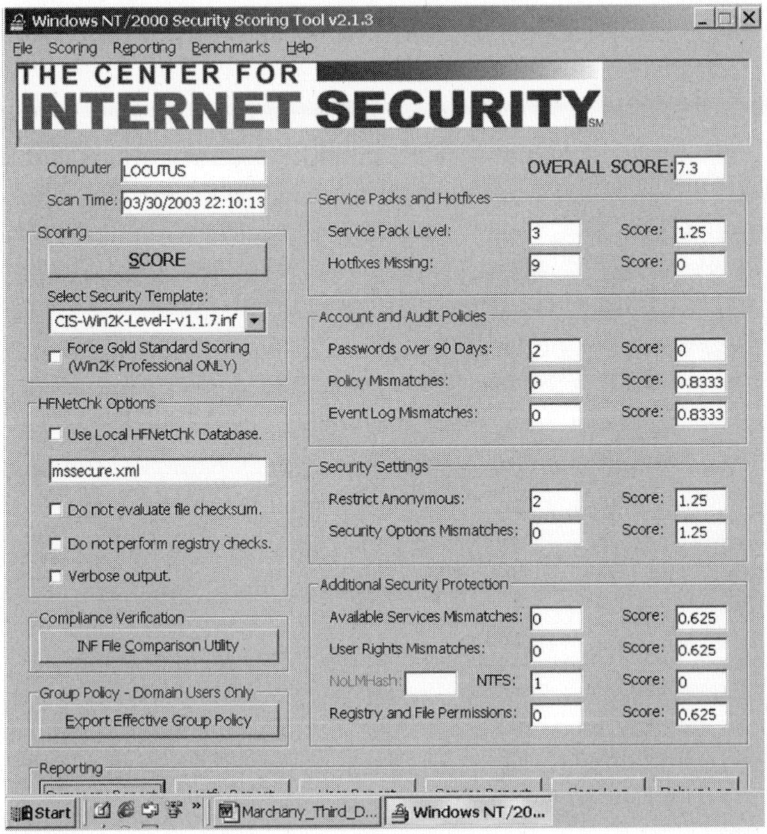

be relaxed. In most cases, vendor software requirements are the primary reason that system security policies are relaxed.

Conclusion

Performing a risk analysis is a necessary first step in assuring the security of campus technology resources. A partnership between IT and auditors on campus acknowledges the common goal of these two groups and can be effective in garnering support for implementing plans to mitigate risks.

Many resources are available to help institutions perform a risk management study. Institutions should select a method to identify and categorize assets and the risks to those assets, and use a simple, replicable process, such as the STAR process, to prioritize assets and risks.

The matrices and scoring tools described or referenced in this chapter provide a quick way for auditors to determine compliance with the institution's standards. The same matrices give systems administrators the status of security controls installed on a particular asset. As an example, the STAR technique simplifies standard risk analysis methods and makes it easier for all departments to provide meaningful information to the institution.

As with other risk management activities, conducting a security risk analysis is not a one-time event. Audits should be performed regularly to ensure compliance with critical security measures and with plans for mitigating risk. Periodic evaluations of the entire IT security program are necessary to maintain agreed-on levels of security.

References

Cassidy, D., and others. "Developing a Strategy to Manage Enterprisewide Risk in Higher Education." Washington, D.C.: National Association of College and Business Officers, 2001.

Jopeck, E. "The Risk Assessment: Five Steps to Better Risk Management Decisions." *Security Awareness Bulletin*, 1997, 3–97, 5–15.

National Infrastructure Protection Center. "Risk Management: An Essential Guide to Protecting Critical Assets." [www.in.gov/c-tasc/whatsnew/ risk_management11-02.pdf]. Nov. 2002.

Qayoumi, M. H. *Mission Continuity Planning: Strategically Assessing and Planning for Threats to Operations*. Washington, D.C.: National Association of College and University Business Officers, 2002.

Siri, L. "Internet Audit Project." [www.viacorp.com/auditing.html]. 1998.

Swanson, M. *Security Self-Assessment Guide for Information Technology Systems*, NIST Special Publication 800–26. Washington, DC. National Institute of Standards and Technology. [csrc.nist.gov/publications/nistpubs/800-26/ sp800-26.pdf]. Nov. 2001.

4

Liability for Negligent Security
Implications for Policy and Practice

Nancy E. Tribbensee

In Lewis Carroll's *Through the Looking Glass*, Alice was puzzled when she noticed that the White Knight had tied a mousetrap to his horse's saddle:

> "I was wondering what the mouse-trap was for," said Alice. "It isn't very likely there would be any mice on the horse's back."
> "Not very likely, perhaps," said the Knight, "but if they *do* come, I don't choose to have them running all about." (Carroll, 1960, p. 298)

Colleges and universities rarely have the luxury of having a White Knight around that is so completely prepared for every risk management contingency. Increasingly tight budgets force administrators to choose among various options to manage risks and provide appropriate security. Requests for resources to enhance computer and network security must compete with a myriad of other legitimate requests, from faculty salaries to the physical security of the campus community. Each decision to spend money on IT security must be justified by balancing the cost and convenience of the mousetrap, the likelihood of encountering mice, and the damage they might do if allowed to run about.

The following discussion focuses on one of the issues that must be considered as resources are allocated to cyberspace security: the risk of legal liability for negligent computer and network security. The purpose of this discussion is to provide information for those administrators who must justify their requests for enhanced security, as well as for those who must decide which requests to grant.

The discussion of legal liability in this chapter is limited to a review of the general principles of negligence law and the influence of the concept of legal duty on policy development. Federal and state statutes that regulate the use, disclosure, and interception of electronic communications and that protect the privacy of the records they hold may contain other sanctions (both civil and criminal) and should be reviewed separately. These statutes are also indirectly relevant to negligence liability insofar as they create expectations in those using information systems. They may also be deemed by a court of law to establish a standard of care to which the entity operating the system will be held for purposes of negligence liability. The reader is referred to Salomon, Cassat, and Thibeau (2003) for a more comprehensive summary of federal and state laws regarding privacy and security in the higher education environment.

Taking an Institutional Perspective on Computer and Network Security

Colleges and universities have considerable experience in evaluating the general risks of campus life and their potential for negligence claims. For example, administrators are generally familiar with claims for physical injuries that can arise from poorly maintained or unsafe premises. In this context, they routinely balance the cost of repairs or additional security against the likelihood of serious harm.

When it comes to electronic and computing resources, various campus constituencies may disagree about the methods used to evaluate risks or to predict the costs to address foreseeable risks. Those who understand information systems and their vulnerabilities may be inclined to devote a greater percentage of resources to protect them. Those whose understanding of these systems is limited to their convenience as a communications tool may never really focus on the risks and consequences of system damage or failure; they may have been lulled into complacency by the successful administration of the system in the past. Decision makers who perceive security risks to be minimal will be less likely to devote resources to address those risks. Among the costs for each campus constituency to consider is the potential for institutional liability if the system fails, is damaged, or is infiltrated by unauthorized users.

Colleges and universities are responsible for maintaining their physical premises in a reasonable manner to avoid foreseeable risks to students, employees, and visitors to campus. They also need to protect institutional property from harm or damage. Administrators recognize that their institutions face potential liability for negligence if they maintain their physical premises in a manner that facilitates foreseeable harm, even if a criminal third party causes the harm. For example, stairwells should be lit so users can see the stairs, and holes in grass playing fields should be filled so athletes and others do not injure themselves. In addition, offices should be locked at night to deter theft, and many student residence halls restrict access after hours to protect students from nonresidents.

Similarly, institutions may be liable for inadequate security that results in loss or damage of information or data or damage to computing networks. Clearly, they may be liable for losses they cause directly. They may also be liable, however, for damage they facilitate through inadequate protection of sensitive or valuable information or data. The administrators who allocate resources and implement policies should be advised of circumstances that can contribute to potential liability both directly and indirectly.

Communication and information systems may be used inadvertently in a manner that compromises system security or damages or destroys information. External forces of nature (for example, floods, tornadoes, and earthquakes) may damage systems or electronically stored records. Stored records may deteriorate over time in such a way that information is lost. Valuable electronic data may become inaccessible over time if devices to read it are not maintained or if the information is not migrated to another more permanent form of storage.

Records stored electronically may be the target of an attack (for example, hacking or a "terrorist" attack). They may contain evidence of a crime or other wrongdoing (for example, stalking, theft, or a copyright violation). Information systems may be used to perpetrate a crime or wrongdoing (for example, harassment or distribution of a worm or virus). These examples support the need for including technology resources and information systems in periodic campus security and liability reviews.

Networked computer resources may also be critical in mitigating risk or avoiding liability. They may provide a means to store data that is safer or more accessible than paper records. They may also provide valuable evidence to be used in the investigation of a crime or other wrongdoing.

How Much Security Is Enough?

"Hackers Seize More Than 50,000 Social Security Numbers from U. of Texas Database" (Read, 2003) and "Hacker Steals Personal Data on Foreign Students at U. of Kansas" (Arnone, 2003). These recent headlines have caught the attention of campuses across the country and sparked discussions of the need to evaluate the security of campus computing systems. Many administrators were already familiar with the allegations that Princeton admissions officers broke into Yale's admissions Web site to check the admission status of applicants who had applied to both Yale and Princeton. Princeton allegedly used information that students provided on its application for admission, such as name, birth date, and Social Security number to access the admissions information on the Yale site. The incident has been the subject of an FBI investigation, and both universities have had to address campus concerns (Zager, 2003).

In light of these incidents, few would argue against the need for security. But how much security is enough? In addition to complying with statutes and other regulatory schema, colleges and universities must evaluate the potential for lawsuits alleging that they were negligent in maintaining computer systems and networks. Just as every physical injury that occurs on campus does not result in institutional liability, not every loss of data will result in a successful negligence claim. More important, essential values of campus life can be lost if college and university administrators are not careful to balance their review of legal liability with important policy considerations. The following discussion is intended to provide information about negligence law in a context that promotes thoughtful policy decisions that protect academic values in the context of electronic campus resources.

Civil Liability

Negligence law provides a mechanism to determine who should bear the risk of loss for some harm or injury that has occurred. Filing a negligence claim is not the only way for someone to recover civil damages for an injury or harm, however. If an institution's failure to maintain adequate security of its information systems results in harm to an individual or damage to records, the injured party may file a civil action for breach of contract or for any of a variety of torts, including invasion of privacy, conversion, defamation, obscenity, harassment, stalking, fraud, identity theft, or negligence. A number of federal and state statutes that regulate electronic communications also provide for criminal sanctions. The reader is referred to Jacobson and Green (2002) for a comprehensive summary of computer crimes.

General Principles of Negligence Law

The focus of this section is limited to the degree to which an institution may be liable under the principles of negligence law in relation to its management of computer systems and electronic resources. By focusing on one element of negligence, the existence of a legal duty, the section will provide guidance to administrators regarding implications for policy development.

Before an institution can be held liable for negligence, the complaining party must prove four separate elements. The four elements required for negligence liability are duty, breach, damage, and causation. To establish *duty*, the complaining party must prove that the institution had a legally recognized duty. Next it must show that the institution *breached* that duty. The complaining party also must prove that it suffered some *harm* or *damage*. Finally, it must show that it was the institution's breach of its legal duty that *caused* the harm or damage. A claim may begin with "My data have been lost," or "Someone accessed my student information without permission," but unless the complaining party goes on to establish all of the other required elements of a negligence claim, the institution will not be liable under negligence law.

The third and fourth elements, that is, damages and causation, are very fact-specific, so they are not discussed here. These elements will need to be analyzed on a case-by-case basis when a loss is alleged to have occurred. The questions of legal duty, both its existence and breach, have particular relevance for administrators deciding on security policies outside of the context of an individual lawsuit, however. Because an understanding of duty can inform the development of policy, it is discussed in more detail here.

Legal Duty and Its Relationship to Security Policy Development

A legally recognized duty can arise in various ways. It can arise from a statutory obligation. It can be created by a contract or promise. It can be assumed in language found in an institutional policy or mission statement. It can be implied from control of facilities or from a special relationship between the parties. It can be implied by the standard of care in the industry.

A duty can take many forms. An injured party may allege that the institution has an absolute duty to prevent all harm or loss from occurring (for example, a proposed duty to protect against all unauthorized access). Courts are very unlikely to impose such an onerous burden on any college or university, however. In keeping with general principles of negligence law, courts will look to the foreseeability of the harm. They are likely to find that an institution has a duty to take reasonable steps to prevent a foreseeable loss. For example, a court might say that a college or university has a duty to institute reasonable security measures to protect electronic records from foreseeable attempts at unauthorized access. The "reasonableness" of the steps taken will be evaluated in light of the value of the data and the potential for harm associated with their loss or unauthorized release (Kenneally, 2002).

An Analogy to Security in Campus Housing

Cases involving security issues that have arisen in campus housing can provide a useful analogy for understanding broader campus security issues. Courts have had multiple opportunities to review claims of negligent security in campus student housing. Like computing systems, student housing is a campus resource that is subject to unauthorized access by outsiders. In addition, some invited guests (authorized users) may behave badly—even criminally—after they are granted authorized access.

In reviewing recent cases of assaults that have occurred in residence halls, for example, different courts have come to very different conclusions on the issue of foreseeability of an assault. The question of the foreseeability of the harm is evaluated in light of the circumstances of the individual case. In *Stanton* v. *University of Maine* (2001), the Supreme Court of Maine found "[t]hat a sexual assault could occur in a dormitory room on a college campus is foreseeable and that fact is evidenced in part by the security measures that the university had implemented" (2001, p. 1050).

In the same year, however, the Iowa Supreme Court came to the opposite conclusion in *Murrell v. Mount St. Clare College*: "A college, or any other kind of landlord . . . is incapable of foreseeing an acquaintance rape that takes place in the private quarters of a student or tenant, unless a specific student or tenant has a past history of such crimes" (2001, p. 4).

By analogy, colleges and university system administrators know that constant attempts are made to access institutional computer systems without authorization, and the persistence of attempts to gain unauthorized access is the motivation for security that is already in place. However, an individual instance of hacking may be unanticipated.

Institutional Responses to Security Breaches

Some intrusion attempts are inspired by the same motivation used to scale Mount Everest: because it is there. Other attempts are more sinister and intend real harm. A recent example that has received much publicity is the theft of medical and other information about military personnel from TriWest Healthcare Alliance in Phoenix, Arizona. In a late 2002 news release (McIntyre, 2003), the president and CEO of TriWest reported the burglary of computer equipment that contained confidential files of more than 500,000 members of the U.S. military. In the press release, TriWest indicates that it does not have knowledge of any use or misuse of the information but acknowledges the potential for "misuse." The press release also indicated that additional security measures have been taken.

Many have speculated that accurate information about security breaches may be difficult to collect. Companies and other large institutions may be reluctant to disclose vulnerabilities for fear of frightening consumers. In addition, they may be concerned about providing too much information to other would-be intruders.

One institutional response to a loss or claim for damages may be to deny the existence of any duty. In litigation, the defendant may have an incentive to deny the existence of any duty to attempt to have the case dismissed or disposed of through a motion for summary judgment. Although this approach has meaning to litigators, it does not assist administrators in making decisions about security before a loss has occurred. In addition, this reasoning does not help administrators make security decisions immediately after a loss has occurred. For example, well before any claims are filed on behalf of military personnel whose information was stolen, Tri-West has committed to "enhancing security." If it had taken the approach that it did not have any duty to safeguard the information, it would not have a legal basis to support enhanced security. Finally, the "no duty" position is not consistent with the personal philosophy of many college and university administrators. They will be more receptive to the position that they have a duty to implement reasonable security procedures. They can then develop a strategy to determine what level of security is reasonable and appropriate and can then develop a protocol for responding to intrusions or loss of data.

Facilitator University Model

In *The Rights and Responsibilities of the Modern University*, Bickel and Lake (1999) advocate a "facilitator university" approach to the analysis of duty in college and university negligence cases. They begin by reviewing recent case law to conclude that courts are holding colleges and universities to the same legal standards as other large institutions. Administrators who believe that higher educational institutions are immune from suit need only contact their institutions' counsel or risk manager (Vinik, 2002).

In providing strategies to manage the risks associated with negligence liability, Bickel and Lake (1999) describe the facilitator university as follows: "When we think of a facilitator, we think of a guide who provides as much support, information, interaction, and control as is reasonably necessary and appropriate to the situation"

(p. 193). They recognize that a major form of university facilitation is the provision of a range of services to the campus community. They also recognize that although many of these services resemble services provided in the private sector, these services have a unique character in the context of the campus environment (1999, p. 194).

Campus computing resources are an excellent example of such a service. Although similar services are available through off-campus providers, campus computing networks are intended to promote education, research, and communication in an environment protected by academic freedom. Extending the facilitation model to computing resources encourages colleges and universities to make all decisions about computer and network security in the context of this larger educational purpose. Impressive, state-of-the-art security measures that pose unacceptable limits on academic use will not be considered appropriate. Insufficient security that threatens the integrity of data or allows unauthorized access by those outside the academic community will also not be acceptable. Decisions should be based on a desire to create an environment conducive to research and learning rather than simply avoiding liability.

Bickel and Lake (1999) initially developed the facilitator university model to address the potential for negligence issues that arise in the context of high-risk student behavior. One feature of the campus computing environment that is analogous to managing student behavior is that both areas challenge the institution to work with individuals who may not recognize that any risk exists and to encourage those individuals to change their behavior. The virtue of the facilitator model is that it operates from an orientation of shared responsibility. In the student arena, the challenge is to help young college students, away from home for the first time, to understand the risks they face from alcohol use. In campus computing, the challenges include helping busy faculty, students, and administrators understand the security needs behind admonitions to change passwords, turn off machines that are not in use, disable unnecessary features, and avoid opening e-mail attachments from unknown sources.

This model is extremely useful as a basis for campus policy development. First, the population that ultimately will be governed by the policy is generally very well educated and will respond better to this approach than to an autocratic dictate to behave differently. Also, it distributes some very important responsibility to those in the best position to manage it. In addition, by promoting a model of shared responsibility, this approach helps remove information technology personnel from a policing role with which they may not be comfortable. Ideally, through ongoing education and peer pressure, coworkers, colleagues, and students will slowly begin to adopt better practices with regard to security. Finally, by educating users on the issues related to security, reasonable expectations are promoted as to the degree of security they can reasonably expect.

To acknowledge the limits of the earlier analogy to campus housing, computing resources present unique challenges. An unauthorized entry into one residence hall does not facilitate unauthorized entry into halls across the country and around the world. Breaches of security in individual computing systems, however, can create the potential for unauthorized access into other systems connected to the first. This greatly expands the class of individuals and entities that may be affected by security decisions and practices.

Without lessening the focus on steps that individuals can take to promote computer and network security, the institution will be in a better position to manage some systemwide risks than will individual users. Awareness created by the shared responsibility model will, however, make it easier for users to understand why certain (often temporarily inconvenient) steps may need to be taken to address a breach of security.

Risk Management and Insurance

In evaluating campus approaches to computer and network security, administrators should consider consulting with the campus risk manager and the entity that provides liability coverage for the institution. These individuals can provide information about the claims experiences of others they insure and the extent of coverage available for information security issues. They may also be excellent sources of information regarding risk management strategies appropriate to the environment.

The Clinton and Bush administrations have worked with the insurance industry to find ways to make cybersecurity insurance more widely available (Krebs, 2003). This is important even for institutions that are self-insured or otherwise already have coverage. As cybersecurity insurance becomes more available and affordable, parties will have an increased incentive to lower costs by implementing security and managing risks. In addition, higher education institutions will have increased opportunities to shift the risk of loss for some security issues to other entities by means of interinstitutional contracts.

Conclusion

Colleges and universities can facilitate their primary education and research missions by managing the risks associated with information technology and cyberspace security by using a model of shared responsibility. Any security review of technology and information resources should consider the value of information stored on systems, the costs to replace that information, and the damage or injury that might result if the information were disclosed to persons not otherwise authorized to access it. In addition, the costs to users of being without the system or having to rely on alternative systems must be considered. Finally, recognizing that various campus constituencies may assess risks and costs differently, a team approach to information security risk management is recommended. The team should include representatives who are intimately familiar with campus communication and information systems, as well as representatives who are close to each of the various users, such as faculty, staff, and students. Legal counsel and institutional risk management personnel should also be included for their perspective on legal liability.

References

Arnone, M. "Hacker Steals Personal Data on Foreign Students at U. of Kansas." [chronicle.com/cgi2-bin/printable_verity.cgi]. Jan. 24, 2003.

Bickel, R. D., and Lake, P. F. *The Rights and Responsibilities of the Modern University: Who Assumes the Risks of College Life?* Durham, N.C.: Carolina Academic Press, 1999.

Carroll, L. *The Annotated Alice: Alice's Adventures in Wonderland and Through the Looking Glass.* New York: New American Library, 1960.

Jacobson, H., and Green, R. "Computer Crimes." *American Criminal Law Review,* 2002, *39,* 273–325.

Kenneally, E. "Who's Liable for Insecure Networks?" *Computer,* 2002, pp. 93–95.

Krebs, B. "White House Pushing Cybersecurity Insurance." [www.washingtonpost.com/ac2/wp-dyn/A55719-2002Jun27]. Jan. 2003.

McIntyre, D. J. "U.S. Attorney for Arizona and TriWest Healthcare Alliance Press Conference to Discuss Identity Theft and TriWest's $100,000 Reward" [www.triwest.com/announcement]. Jan. 2003.

Murrell v. *Mount St. Clare College,* 2001 WL 16778766 (S.D. Iowa 2001).

Read, B. "Hackers Seize More than 50,000 Social Security Numbers From U. of Texas Database." [chronicle.com/cgi2-bin/printable_verity.cgi]. Mar. 7, 2003.

Salomon, K. D., Cassat, P. C., and Thibeau, B. E. "IT Security for Higher Education: A Legal Perspective." [www.educause.edu/ir/library/pdf/CSD2746.pdf]. Mar. 20, 2003.

Stanton v. *University of Maine,* 773 A.2d 1045 (Me. 2001).

Vinik, F. *Intellectual Property and Cyberspace: A Risk and Resource Guide for Educational Institutions.* Chevy Chase, Md.: United Educators, 2002.

Zager, M. "Oops! Princeton Snoops on Yale Applicants, FBI Steps In." [wysiwyg://42/www.newsfactor.com/perl/story/18782.html]. Jan. 2003.

5

Policy Development for Information Security

Mark Bruhn and Rodney Petersen

Successful efforts to improve security on various campuses have not followed a single formula. In some cases, it took a serious security incident to capture the attention of senior management and provide the impetus for change. In other cases, the leadership and support of the chief information officer or another senior official was the critical factor. Although common ingredients can be found, the experiences of colleges and universities across the country suggest there have been multiple paths taken and varying paces at which institutions are working to meet their security goals.

This chapter describes the importance of policy development for information security and different ways within a college or university setting to get the desired results.

Security Strategies and Plans

A common plea among many IT staff and data stewards revolves around development of an "information security policy" for the institution. Initially, these constituents are not expecting or demanding the kind of detailed institutional policies and procedures described later in this chapter. Rather, they desire some demonstration of a commitment on the part of the senior administration to a program of improved information security. Indeed, a helpful security policy might take the form of a statement of strategic direction or symbolic expression of organizational value accorded to an information security program. This approach is consistent with general policy processes, inasmuch as policies are often (and, if not, should be) validated by strategies or plans established or endorsed by executives and other institutional decision makers. Such a statement related to IT security needs only to identify improving security of the technology environment as a priority and demonstrate a corresponding commitment by directing or encouraging allocation of the necessary institutional resources. The statement does not need to be—and should not be—clouded by mechanical details designed to dictate technologies that must be employed and standards that must be followed. Those standards should be set later and be supported by the policy statement.

The vision for any information security program should be to support the attainment of institutional goals and priorities. It is easy to sometimes confuse security as the end goal instead of as an activity among many others that supports the purposes for which the enterprise exists—teaching and learning, research and discovery, and outreach and service. The goals of an information security program are to ensure the confidentiality, integrity, and availability of information and organizational resources. Information security, like technology in general, must be approached as an enabler of institutional processes and a means to support attainment of the broader mission.

Security Policies and Procedures

Although there is a close relationship between "plans" and "policies" as described in the previous section, a strategic or tactical plan is not a substitute for a formal statement of institutional intention or direction that is typically contained within a formal institutional policy. The term *policy* can mean different things to different people. As used in the previous section, it can represent the strategic direction or operating philosophy of an organization. *Policy* is also a term used to describe legislative and regulatory developments, also known as *public policy*. However, in the context of operational statements or directions, colleges and universities tend to think in terms of *institutional policies*. This section outlines elements of institutional policies and other supporting documents, describes an effective policy development process, reviews some sample security policy issues, and explores the model set of authorities for information security at Indiana University (IU).

Elements of Institutional Policies

If the goal of institutional policies is to direct individual behavior and guide institutional decisions, then the effectiveness of formal policy statements will depend on their readability and usefulness. Many colleges and universities suffer from the lack of a common and consistent approach or format for writing organizational policies. Policy development is often confused and sometimes derailed because of the misunderstanding or misuse of terms with important meanings to a professional policy administrator, legal counsel, and others. The outline below suggests some common elements.

Rationale or Purpose

The rationale or purpose statement expresses why the policy is being written. The rationale or purpose may also contain or cross-reference "background" materials or more explanatory details regarding legal, regulatory, or other factors that led to the development of the policy.

Policy Statement

The policy statement should be a concise statement of what the policy is intended to accomplish. The policy should only be a one- or two-sentence description of general organizational intent with respect to the specific topic of the policy. The policy statement should be general enough to provide some flexibility to accommodate new circumstances or periodic changes in technology. Policies are statements that reflect the philosophies, attitudes, or values of an organization related to a specific issue. Procedures, guidelines, checklists, and standards all must implement, reflect, and support the applicable policy or policies.

Scope of Policy

The scope of the policy can set important parameters such as to whom the policy will apply (for example, faculty, staff, students, and guests) and to what (for example, paper and electronic records, information and computer assets).

Procedures

The procedures detail how the policy statement will be accomplished. Procedures contain one or more sentences describing how to accomplish a task or reach a goal. The specified actions are generally mandatory for the specific situation. More explanatory text is usually involved. A sequence is not necessary but sometimes is important. Procedures may include information on how to report computer security incidents. Procedures may also describe enforcement provisions or methods for appeal.

Roles and Responsibilities

The procedures may contain details about who is responsible for what. The policy should also identify who is responsible for enforcement or compliance and who will provide interpretations in the event of the need for clarification or when there is a dispute.

Definitions

Policies should be precise and easy to understand. Sometimes terms will need to be defined to clarify meaning. However, the policy should attempt to convey messages in simple yet precise terms; excessive definitions may make a policy document unreadable or subject to greater scrutiny when a particular term critical to a dispute is left undefined.

References

Other existing policies or organizational documents might exist that complement, supplement, or help explain the provisions contained within the current policy. References to other policies, guidelines, checklists, standards, organizational documents, and citations to statutory or regulatory items can improve the usefulness of the policy.

Guidelines

Guidelines contain information about how to accomplish some task or reach a specific goal. They are provided as suggestions; in other words, they are not mandatory, but they are a good idea. That is, they represent "best practices" and, although alternate actions might be available and might work, those being provided have proven to be the fastest, cheapest, and so on.

Checklists

Checklists contain one or more statements dictating how to accomplish a task, that is, "commands." The items are applicable to an immediate circumstance and mandatory in that defined situation. Checklists are typically immediately at hand and written in simple language with no amplifying text. The sequence is always important. Flowcharts are also used as a method for conveying similar information.

Standards

Standards are statements dictating the state of affairs or action in a particular circumstance. They establish a rule from a recognized authority, with no deviation allowed.

Several helpful books and resources are available that describe typical security policy elements and include sample statements for security that correspond with the areas identified above (Barman, 2002; Desman, 2002; Joint Information Systems Committee, 2001; King and others, 2001; Nichols, Ryan, and Ryan, 2000; Peltier, 2001,

2002; Tudor, 2001; U.S. Department of Education, 1998; Walker and Cavanaugh, 1998; Wood, 2002).

Policy Process

Some institutions have developed a "policy on policies" that provides an institutional statement and set of procedures about the elements of institutional policies, who develops them, and how they get approved (see "Formulation and Issuance of Policies" from Cornell University at www.univco.cornell.edu/policy/pop.for.html and "Guide to Writing University Policy" from the University of Minnesota at www.fpd.finop.umn.edu/groups/ppd/documents/information/Guide_to_Writing.cfm). The benefit of a formal approach is that it makes policy development consistent and recognizes policy approval authorities.

The Association of College and University Policy Administrators (ACUPA) promotes a document entitled Policy Development Process with Best Practices (2001) that contains the following stages: (1) identify issues, (2) conduct analysis, (3) draft language, (4) get approvals, (5) determine distribution/education, (6) solicit evaluation and review, and (7) plan measurement and compliance. Stages 1 and 2 are considered "predevelopment," whereas stages 3 through 5 are part of "development" and stages 6 and 7 are "maintenance."

The process recommended by ACUPA contains several useful features for the development of security policies. First, issue identification as a proactive component should build on a security risk analysis as discussed in Chapter Three of this book, including the identification of existing information or data security policies.

Second, the identification of the policy owner, policy path, and policy development team is critical to ensuring the ultimate success of the security policy. Views are mixed about whether or not to include legal counsel as part of the drafting team or whether legal counsel should only be a part of a subsequent review process to determine the legal sufficiency of policy documents. Allowing legal counsel to work with the policy early on leads to the possible danger that a security policy will be written in terms too complex for its intended audience. However, lawyers should be knowledgeable about security requirements under federal or state law.

Third, drafting language and getting approvals is a strategic and political process at most institutions. Because of the urgency of computer and network security for our institutions, it may be more expedient to issue "guidelines" or "interim policies and procedures" to protect assets and ensure legal compliance while using shared governance processes for formal review and adoption of institutional policy.

Fourth, education and awareness of security issues and the corresponding policies and procedures is critical. A policy that no one knows about or a policy that is not followed can do more harm than good.

Finally, the maintenance stage underscores the importance of regularly evaluating security policies to ensure that they are effective and evolve as vulnerabilities change and technology evolves.

Security Policy Issues

Writing "the" security policy to cover all of the possible issues and considerations is an often intimidating and formidable task. It should come as no surprise that security policies come in every shape and size depending on the complexity of the organization, pressing requirements for legal and regulatory compliance, or resources available to devote to policy development. Although there is a tendency to want a "template" or model policy to follow, there is recognition that policies must be designed to meet the needs of the affected communities, while keeping an eye on the importance of education and awareness of the resulting policy elements. Yet there is a need for a broad understanding of the policy issues to be addressed and at the same time a need to access a robust collection of policies and policy development resources on which to draw. For the latter, the reader is referred to the EDUCAUSE/Internet2 Computer and Network Security Task Force Web site (www.educause.edu/security) and the

SANS Security Policy Project Web site (www.sans.org/resources/policies) as two excellent sources of policy collections and related resources on IT security policy issues. Comprehensive outlines of what to include in a security policy are available at www.sans.org/rr/policy/policy.php (Farnsworth, 2000) and www.boran.com/security/IT1x-6.html ("IT Security Cookbook," 2000).

Acceptable Use Policy

Colleges and universities have generally addressed computer security issues through their acceptable use policies. A typical acceptable use policy contains provisions about unauthorized access to computer systems and files, the need to safeguard user IDs and passwords, what levels of privacy to expect, and general prohibitions regarding illegal activities, including computer crimes. It is possible to modify an existing acceptable use policy to include additional responsibilities for security not previously included. However, acceptable use policies are targeted toward end users of computer systems and establish parameters for appropriate use of computing resources. They are considered a "component of the overall information security policy" (Mandia and Prosise, 2001, p. 463). They do not typically stress how users, technology staff, and departments have to behave in order to secure systems, nor do they provide guidance on security practices or how to best maintain systems.

Other Policy Issues

A number of specific policy issues touch on computer and network security. A comprehensive security policy might attempt to address as many as possible of the topics listed below in one collective document (see the security guide for San Francisco State University Division of Information Technology at www.sfsu.edu/~helpdesk/docs/rules/security.htm) or attempt to chip away at each topic individually in support of broader policy objectives (see the departmental security contact policy for the University of California, Berkeley, at socrates.berkeley.edu:2002/contacts.html). In any event, institutions should review their policies, procedures, and practices to see whether the following topics are addressed:

- Audits and risk assessments

- Authentication and enterprise directory

- Authorization and access management

- Backups and disaster recovery

- Business continuity

- Computer disposal and disk wiping

- Confidentiality and nondisclosure

- Configuration standards for desktop computers

- Departmental security contacts

- Domain name system service

- Encryption, public key infrastructure, and private key escrow

- Filtering and intrusion detection

- Firewall implementation

- Hardware and software asset inventory

- Incident classification and reporting

- Incident response team and protocols

- Laptops and portable equipment security

- Logging and monitoring practices

- Password protection

- Physical access to data centers and other critical sites

- Physical security of equipment

- Privacy of personal information

- Privacy of user files and content

- Remote access to systems and resources

- Responding to law enforcement requests

- Safeguarding financial information

- Scanning for vulnerabilities

- Software licensing and compliance

- Supervision and training of staff

- Virtual private networks

- Virus prevention and detection

- Wireless communication

Examples of policies or further description of the security issues identified above are available from the EDUCAUSE/Internet2 Computer and Network Security Task Force (www.educause.edu/security) or SANS (www.sans.org/resources/policies) policy Web sites.

Model Authority for Information Security

A well-publicized data exposure incident involving Indiana University's bursar's office in February 2001 shed light on the fact that a concerted effort between university departments and the central IT policy and security staff is necessary to ensure that all aspects are considered in responding to an incident. During this particular incident, the common complaint by affected individuals—and the aspect of most interest to the media—was that the length of time it took to notify the potentially affected individuals was too long—letters were sent twenty-five days after the exposure was recognized.

During the annual report on the state of security from the vice president for information technology and CIO (VPIT/CIO) to the IU Board of Trustees in May 2001, detailed information about the cause and the response to the bursar's office incident was presented. The presentation also included information about the likely lack of preparedness of IU departments to prevent similar incidents and their capability to react appropriately should other incidents occur. Although some in the IU community suggested that the VPIT/CIO had the implied authority to take steps to improve IT security across all departments and campuses and to become directly involved in any required response, an explicit recognition of this authority by the governing board was deemed necessary and appropriate. A resolution, drafted jointly by the VPIT/CIO and university general counsel, was presented to the Board of Trustees' Finance and Audit Committee. However, after brief deliberation the board members chose to make the language stronger; indeed the final resolution *directed* . . . "the Office of the Vice President for Information Technology and CIO to develop and implement policies necessary to minimize the possibility of unauthorized access to Indiana University's information technology infrastructure regardless of the Indiana University office involved; and . . . draw[ing] upon the experience and expertise and resources of other University offices (including the Office of Internal Audit), to assume leadership, responsibility, and control of responses to unauthorized access to Indiana University's information technology infrastructure, unauthorized disclosure of electronic information and computer security breaches regardless of the Indiana University office involved" (Indiana University, 2001). The entire text of the resolution can be viewed at www.itpo.iu.edu/Resolution.html.

Closely following the adoption of this resolution, another well-publicized incident occurred involving the Indiana University School of Music in June 2001. Although it is difficult to quantify the effect that the resolution and the more active involvement of the central IT security office may have had on the overall response to that incident, it is clear that the response was much smoother and much quicker. As one measure, notification of the potentially affected individuals, which included some individuals external to the university, took only seven days. In any case, after the two incidents and passage of the resolution, consultations with the central IT policy and security officers by department managers and technicians on security vulnerabilities, threats, and similar issues increased dramatically and are now commonplace.

This formal conferring of authority is analogous to the formal charge conferred on internal audit departments, which are generally separated from functions and operations and are at least partly responsible to the governing body of the institution. The resolution and the authority conveyed to the IU IT policy and security offices has smoothed significantly the path to an overall emphasis and improvement in IT security at Indiana University.

Conclusion

The need to improve computer and network security will make the combined strategies of security plans and policies an essential element of institutional processes that manage data or rely on computer networks. Planning for the protection of information resources and computer assets is no longer just the responsibility of the IT organization. The organizational value of networked information combined with the inherent risks in computer networks make IT risk management an increasingly important institutional priority. The development and enforcement of organizational policies requires engagement and support of the executive leadership as well.

References

Association of College and University Policy Administrators. "Policy Development Process with Best Practices." [www.umd.edu/acupa/projects/process]. Apr. 2001.

Barman, S. *Writing Information Security Policies*. Boston: New Riders, 2002.

Desman, M. B. *Building an Information Security Awareness Program*. Boca Raton, Fla.: Auerbach Publications, 2002.

Farnsworth, W. "What Do I Put in a Security Policy?" [www.sans.org/rr/policy/ policy.php]. Apr. 2000.

Indiana University. "Resolution of the Trustees of Indiana University Regarding the Leadership, Responsibility, and Security of IU's Information Technology Infrastructure." [www.itpo.iu.edu/Resolution.html]. May 2001.

"IT Security Cookbook." [www.boran.com/security/IT1x-6.html]. July 2000.

Joint Information Systems Committee. "Developing an Information Security Policy." [www.jisc.ac.uk/index.cfm?name=jcas_papers_security]. Feb. 2001.

King, C. M., and others. *Security Architecture: Design, Deployment and Operations*. New York: Osborne/McGraw-Hill, 2001.

Mandia, K., and Prosise, C. *Incident Response: Investigating Computer Crime*. New York: Osborne/McGraw-Hill. 2001.

Nichols, R. K., Ryan, D. J., and Ryan, J.J.C.H. *Defending Your Digital Assets Against Hackers, Crackers, Spies and Thieves*. Washington, D.C.: McGraw-Hill, 2000.

Peltier, T. R. *Information Security Risk Analysis*. Boca Raton, Fla.: Auerbach Publications, 2001.

Peltier, T. R. *Information Security Policies, Procedures, and Standards: Guidelines for Effective Information Security Management*. Boca Raton, Fla.: Auerbach Publications, 2002.

Tudor, J. K. *Information Security Architecture: An Integrated Approach to Security in the Organization*. Boca Raton, Fla.: Auerbach Publications, 2001.

U.S. Department of Education. "Safeguarding Your Technology: Practical Guidelines for Electronic Information Security." Washington D.C.: National Center for Education Statistics. [nces.ed.gov/pubs98/98297.pdf]. Sept. 1998.

Walker, K. M., and Cavanaugh, L. Croswhite. *Computer Security Policies and SunScreen Firewalls*. Palo Alto, Calif.: Sun Microsystems Press, 1998.

Wood, C. C. *Information Security Policies Made Easy*. (9th ed.) Houston, Tex.: PentaSafe Security Technologies, Inc., 2002.

6

Security Architecture

Jack Suess

The focus of this chapter will be on how institutions can use an IT security architecture to "build in" security as we plan, design, and deploy the networks, computers, middleware, and applications that make up our IT infrastructure.

It is important to acknowledge at the beginning that there is no single solution for an IT security architecture that will work across the thousands of higher education institutions in existence today; however, there are common elements of an IT security architecture that each campus should consider when developing its security plan. These common elements include network security, computer (or "host") security, middleware and directory services, and application-based security. An IT security architecture should be integrated with the broader IT plan for the campus and support those IT initiatives proposed in the plan. In fact, many aspects of IT security architecture, such as the use of a central directory for authentication, can be enabling technologies that facilitate the development of a broad range of IT initiatives (Barton and others, 2001).

A second acknowledgment is that our IT infrastructure is constantly evolving. As a result, our security architecture must be adapted to keep pace. This is a curse in that our work is never complete, but also a blessing in that we can opportunistically replace technology in accordance with our IT plan and at the same time enhance security.

The remainder of this chapter discusses each element of an IT security architecture. Purposely, this chapter is written at a high level and is not directed to network engineers and system administrators. An excellent primer for technical personnel is RFC 2196—"Site Security Handbook" developed by the Internet Engineering Task Force (Fraser, 1997).

Network Security

Network security architecture is the planning and design of the campus network to reduce security risks in accordance with the institution's risk analysis and security policies. It focuses on reducing security risks and enforcing policy through the design and configuration of firewalls, routers, and other network equipment.

Network security is important because it is one of the means to enforce the policies and procedures developed by the institution to protect information. It is often referred to as the "front door" in broader discussions of IT security. To the extent that you can block network access to a computer, you "lock" the door and provide better protection for that computer and its contents.

Traditional network design has focused on creating a secure network perimeter around the organization and strategically placing a firewall at the point where the network is connected to the Internet. For higher education, this traditional design is problematic; our constituents need access from off campus to a large number of machines and services on campus. In addition, because we have many computers on our campus that we cannot implicitly trust, we also must be concerned about security threats from inside the perimeter protected by a traditional firewall. These design issues require a different approach to network security. Although it is impossible to do justice to the topic of network design in a few pages, there are some best practices that I feel universities should focus on in terms of network design:

Step 1: Eliminate Network Components That Still Use Shared Ethernet

Shared Ethernet switches (or hubs) were developed more than a decade ago to interconnect multiple computers and networks. These hubs retransmit all network traffic to all computers connected to that hub. The security implication is that if one computer has its security compromised it can be used to monitor network traffic coming from any other computer that shares the same hub. This could expose passwords and other sensitive information. Today, switched Ethernet, which isolates traffic intended for one computer from the view of others on the same switch, is very inexpensive and, hence, it is worth the cost of replacing older hubs.

Step 2: Embrace and Implement the Concept of Defense and Use Multiple Firewalls Within Your Network

Commercial and Linux-based firewalls are inexpensive enough that you can deploy these in multiple locations as needed. It is still beneficial to have a firewall separating your institutional network from the connection to the Internet. This firewall, called a *border firewall*, will provide a minimal level of protection for all computers on your network. The major benefit of this firewall is that it allows your network and security staff to quickly block external access should a threat arise, such as when the "SQL worm" was launched in January 2003 ("Safe SQL Slammer Worm Attack Mitigation," 2003). In addition to the border firewall, consider adding internal firewalls to protect areas that require different levels of security. For example, placing a firewall between the network segments containing the computers that operate the institutional business systems allows the institution to provide more restrictive security for those computers. Other areas that firewalls can strengthen include residential networks and research labs. Each firewall can have different access controls, support different security policies, and allow for distributed administration— all of which are essential to success in academia (Gray, 2003).

Step 3: Implement Intrusion Detection Systems at Key Points Within Your Network to Monitor Threats and Attacks

An *intrusion detection system* (IDS) looks at the incoming network traffic for patterns that can signify that a person is probing your network for vulnerable computers. The IDS can also look at traffic leaving your institution for patterns that might indicate that a computer's security has been compromised. This probing from off campus is usually the first step in attempting to compromise the security of a computer on your network. IDSs historically have produced daily reports showing what security vulnerabilities were being targeted the day before.

Some vendors are now integrating the IDS with the firewall and renaming these *intrusion prevention systems*. When a threat is identified, the IDS automatically works with the firewall to adjust the firewall rules to protect the computers on the network. IDS products are broadly available through commercial vendors and the open-source community. At my institution, we use an open-source product named Snort (Grimes, 2002; Roesch, 2003).

Step 4: Implement a Virtual Private Network Concentrator for Off-Campus and Wireless Access

A *virtual private network* (VPN) uses special software on each computer, called a VPN client, to encrypt network traffic from that computer to a VPN concentrator on the institution's network. Using a VPN allows a member of your institution to securely connect to campus computers from an off-campus computer. The VPN will establish an encrypted connection that allows the off-campus computer to appear as if it were part of your internal campus network, thereby granting access to resources that may be blocked by a border firewall (Frasier, 2002).

Many institutions are actively implementing wireless networks on campus. Wireless networks can create many security considerations because their signals typically are shared over a broad area. In particular, wireless networks are very much akin to shared Ethernet and may be susceptible to surreptitious monitoring of network traffic. You should encrypt your wireless network traffic to eliminate the risk of others on that same network viewing your network traffic. Because a VPN does this, it is very effective in improving security on wireless networks ("Wireless Security and VPN," 2001).

Step 5: Measure and Report Network Traffic Statistics for the Computers on Your Network That Are Using the Most Bandwidth

Measuring the number of bytes a computer sends and receives to the Internet can help you identify computers that have been compromised. Often, computers that are compromised on campus are used to store large data files (for example, copyrighted music, videos, or software) for others to download. When this happens the computer that was compromised will normally experience a much higher volume of network traffic than normal and will often become one of the largest users of the network. Reviewing the list of top "talkers" for computers that are not normally so active can offer indications that a machine has suffered a security incident (Dunn, 2001).

———————

Although none of these steps by themselves will guarantee security, collectively they provide a good starting point for improving campus network security. As we shall see next, once a computer has been compromised it can be used for a variety of dangerous practices.

Host-Based Security

A computer, often referred to as a *host*, is often the target of hackers. Once a computer has its security compromised, a number of bad things can happen: the computer can be used as file storage for groups sharing illegal material, sensitive information stored on the computer (such as Social Security numbers or credit card information) can be accessed and released, the host may be used as an intermediary to probe other machines for security flaws, or the machine may be used to launch an outright attack on other systems. Because they are often targets, securing the computers—that is, host-based security—is an important part of our IT security architecture.

Universities are often required to have networks that are much more open than other types of organizations to allow collaboration and access by students and faculty from off campus. As a result, computers connected to our campus networks are often more susceptible to hackers than computers in corporate networks. In tests at the University of Maryland, Baltimore County (UMBC), that have been confirmed in similar tests by other universities, we have attached machines running standard versions of Linux and Windows 2000 on our network and timed how long it took for the machine to have its security compromised. In all of the tests, the machines had their security compromised within the day; in fact, often this happened within hours! This occurred because hackers believe higher education institutions are easy targets and probe university networks for computers with security vulnerabilities.

Fortunately, host-based security can be accomplished through good system administration practices, such as maintaining up-to-date virus protection, making certain that the operating system software is configured properly, and ensuring that all of the latest security patches are installed. The challenge is that most campuses have thousands, if not tens of thousands, of computers on campus—most controlled by individuals outside of the central IT organization with little or no training in good system administration practices. I next discuss practices that institutions should promote to enhance host-based security.

Step 1: Establish Virus Protection with an Automated Update Service on All Critical Systems

Computer viruses and worms were the most common security problem during 2000–2002 (Briney, 2002). Although viruses can be written for any operating system, most are written to reach the widest audience and thus exploit security flaws in Microsoft products (Word, Excel, Internet Explorer, and the various versions of Windows). Because these products are among the most heavily used at universities, establishing virus protection on computers using Microsoft products is critical.

New viruses can spread very rapidly; it is important to select a virus product that will allow you to get frequent, automated updates to the virus protection software. Most virus protection products provide a version of their product that can be centrally managed by the institution. This allows the institution to automatically update all computers running the virus protection software at one time. Although this option is more expensive, without this automatic update a virus may strike and do considerable damage before people have updated their virus protection software. Because today's viruses spread through the Internet, by e-mail, and through the Web, they can quickly spread on campus. During one particular virus and worm outbreak, the NIMDA worm, UMBC measured 200,000 NIMDA virus probes from off-campus in one day ("CERT Advisory," 2001).

Step 2: Perform a Risk Assessment to Identify the Most Important Computers to Protect

Almost all institutions have more computers than they can properly protect. In designing a host-based security plan, the first step is to perform a risk assessment (see Chapter Three) to determine which hosts are the most important to protect and to focus first on those computers. In general, this will include computers that provide critical IT functions such as administrative systems, course management systems, e-mail, and Web servers. It should also include computers that contain sensitive information that needs to be protected, such as staff computers used in departments such as the bursar or registrar's office.

Finally, safeguarding research computers used by faculty may be very important as well. Prioritize the computers to protect by risk to the institution.

Step 3: Use a Network Scanning Utility to Create a Profile for Each Computer Identified in Step 2

In this step you create a profile of each computer you identified in step 2, showing the operating system and the different services accessible through the network.

Generally, each network service on a machine is associated with a specific TCP/IP port number (for example, Telnet is port 22, e-mail is port 25, and so on) (Postel et al., 2003). At a small institution it may be possible to examine the machines individually and get this information, but most campuses will want to use an automated tool to detect this information.

Commercial tools such as the Internet Scanner from ISS ("Internet Security Systems," 2003) or public domain software such as Nmap ("Nmap—Network Mapping Software," 2003) can be used to classify machines by operating system and the network services they are running. These tools work by scanning your network and looking for computers that respond. For each computer that responds, they check to see what network services are running and attempt to identify the version of the software. They can also be configured to look for and report known vulnerabilities for each computer.

Step 4: Disable the Network Services That Are Not Needed on the Computers Identified in Step 3; Consider Running a Host-Based Firewall on Your Computer to Block Unwanted Network Traffic

The default configuration for many operating systems is to have the most-common network services enabled. As a result, most machines are running network-based services such as a Web server, database server, or file sharing services that might not be necessary. One good tool for analyzing your system is the CISECURITY toolkit developed by the Center for Internet Security ("The Center for Internet Security," 2003). This toolkit is easy to use and analyzes your system for potential security concerns against different baseline configurations. By disabling unnecessary network services on a computer, you eliminate potential security problems associated with that service that could jeopardize the entire computer.

One newer solution that is gaining favor is to implement host-based firewalls. A *host-based firewall* is software that runs on each computer and is analogous to a network firewall, but it protects a single computer. It requires network traffic coming to the computer to meet certain rules before it is processed (Gwaltney, 2001).

During the next few years, many predict that host-based firewalls will play an important role; however, at present they can be problematic in that they can generate many time-consuming false alarms. Until vendors provide better configuration management capabilities so these can be run from a central place, they will be difficult to deploy across the enterprise. However, using these judiciously for machines that require additional protection may be a viable choice today.

Step 5: Monitor Security Alerts and Develop Mechanisms for Quickly Patching Systems

Dozens of security alert services are available to track security problems. At UMBC, we use the Bugtrak mailing list to track security alerts ("Bugtrak Mailing List Archive," 2003). It is critical that some staff member(s) be assigned to monitor these security alerts. Once a security alert is announced, you can consult your computer profiles generated in step 3 to see what critical machines are vulnerable and work to get the security patch installed on those machines.

If the machines you are tracking number in the thousands, you must look at tools that can help automate the process of updating the machines. Many free as well as commercial tools are available that can assist with this task. The important thing is to make certain your staff has a plan for updating these machines rapidly when a security alert is announced.

One response to security alerts used at many schools is to reset their border firewall to block off-campus access to certain network services if it is believed that many machines will be vulnerable to a new threat until the staff can patch all of the machines susceptible to that problem. Although this may have an impact on some off-campus usage, it may be preferable to letting the machines have their security compromised and dealing with all the consequences.

Step 6: Create a Centralized System Logging Service

All major operating systems provide support for system logging. These system logs record each time a network service is accessed and the success or failure of that access. Usually the record contains a time stamp, some identifying information, and the network service accessed. By default, these system logs are written to the local disk on the computer providing that network service; however, you can configure most systems to also write their logs to a central server via the network.

By centralizing the system logging service, a security officer can accumulate systems logs from hundreds of machines and look at patterns of unusual activity across those machines. An additional benefit of central logging is that if a machine is compromised, the log entries leading up to that compromise will not be lost. This can be very important when examining the cause of a security compromise and looking for other computers that might be affected. Clear policies and procedures regarding the capture, retention, and use of system logs are essential to protect the privacy of those using the systems.

Step 7: Develop a Central Authentication Service to Replace Host-Based Password Files

Host-based password files are notoriously insecure. Invariably users choose passwords that are associated with words or people, things often found in a dictionary. Although most operating systems encrypt the password files, the encryption algorithms are well known. Simple tools are available that allow hackers to go through a dictionary of words and compare the results of encrypting that word until a match is found against the encrypted password. These tools, such as L0phtCrack (Semjanov, 2003), make it easy to gain many user passwords once a machine is compromised.

Developing a centralized security service, such as Kerberos (Kohl and Neumann, 1993), removes user passwords from each

machine and eliminates the ability of someone to decrypt the password files stored on the local computer. Kerberos is available for most
versions of UNIX, Linux, Macintosh OS/X, and Windows 2000/XP
and is free.

The Role of Middleware and Campus Directories

The Internet2 Middleware working group defines *middleware* as a
layer of software between the network and the applications (Klingenstein, 2003). This software provides services such as identification, authentication, authorization, group membership, and security.
Middleware provides the linkage, or "glue," among individuals,
hosts, networks, and the applications deployed. In this section, I
discuss how middleware facilitates security and is a key component
in campus security architecture.

In the past year magazines such as *InfoSecurity, Information Week,*
and *Network Computing* have all listed "identity management" as
one of the key challenges facing organizations (Yasin, 2002). *Identity management* provides automated mechanisms for managing
accounts: creation, deactivation, and deletion. Identity management also supports the varied roles that people have in higher education. For instance, I can be a staff member teaching a course and
also taking a course and thus be a member of the staff, faculty, and
student groups. The key to identity management is building an
enterprise directory linked to your campus business systems: student,
human resources, alumni, and admissions. The enterprise directory
provides authentication services (Am I person X?) and facilitates
authorization information (Am I a member of group Y that has
the authority to use service Z?). Often the authentication component of the enterprise directory is linked to an existing authentication service, such as Kerberos, if one is available for use. If not, the
directory can provide authentication services. It is critical that
the security of the campus directory itself be managed very carefully.

The Internet2 Middleware initiative developed a business case
for implementing middleware in higher education. This document

identified twenty-four uses and applications that were facilitated by the existence of middleware (Barton and others, 2001). More than half of the applications were related to network security, authentication, or controlling authorized use of resources, including portals, VPN access, wireless authentication, and self-service network registration for residential students.

One of the most basic and important security challenges every institution faces is managing user accounts and passwords. Without a directory, a member of the institution can end up with numerous usernames and passwords. When people have multiple accounts, this creates frustration and often leads to poor passwords (passwords that can be easily guessed through a dictionary attack as discussed earlier). For the institution, removing access for an individual when he or she leaves the campus is a tremendous challenge because you have to remove that individual from dozens of application-specific password files. Having these applications use the enterprise directory for authentication provides a single authoritative source for authentication across applications. In the event the individual leaves the institution or you must disable an account for some reason, this can be done in one place, the enterprise directory.

From these examples it should be apparent that middleware is an essential piece of our security architecture. It can also greatly facilitate the development of portals, enterprise resource packages, Web-based services, and so forth by centrally managing identities. Campuses beginning these projects should look at creating a middleware environment that furthers their security architecture in addition to meeting the needs of that project.

Applications and Central Services

A common, but critical security problem today is that many applications and services still send usernames and passwords unencrypted over the network, where they may be captured by hackers who have broken into another computer on the network. As a result you have to assume that any person that used that service has a compromised password. At the least, all users must be contacted and required to change their passwords ("San Diego Super Computer Advisory," 1997).

Common, everyday services that send unencrypted passwords include e-mail, Telnet (provides user access to remote computers), and FTP (transfers files from one computer to another). For most institutions, e-mail is the most heavily used application on campus. If your central e-mail servers have their security compromised, the passwords of thousands of people can be found in just one day.

Solutions have been available for a few years that provide these services by sending encrypted passwords over the network. Although changing software configurations is a major effort in user education, every campus should be working toward replacing these common applications with their "secure" counterparts, as shown in Table 6.1. (A good example is the "University of Colorado Encrypted Authentication Standards," 2003.)

Another source of security problems is Web-based applications that maintain separate usernames and accounts for each user or that don't utilize encryption for sending information from the users' browser to the Web server ("The OpenSSL Project," 2003). In some cases these Web-based applications use the same username that is used by campus servers but maintain separate password files.

Unfortunately, many people will use the same password for all of these applications without understanding that many of these applications don't have strong security. The best solution is associated with middleware: develop a campus-based Web authentication

Table 6.1. Unencrypted Versus Encrypted Applications.

Unencrypted Application	Encrypted Application
Telnet	Secure Shell (SSH)
E-mail	E-mail over Secure Sockets Layer (SSL)
FTP	Secure Copy (SCP)

system that uses the enterprise directory, referred to as a Web initial sign-on (WebISO). By developing a WebISO, Web-based application developers can leverage the enterprise directory and use one central source for authentication. The Internet2 Middleware initiative has software available for institutions that want to develop a WebISO on campus (Dors, 2003).

As we look to the future, we can see that distributed security across multiple institutions will become increasingly important. This is already an issue for scientists using the national supercomputer centers funded by the National Science Foundation and will become an issue for access to online content providers used by our libraries. We are reaching the limits of what we can expect people to handle when it comes to accounts and passwords. Much of the time all of the information we need is an assertion from a trusted party that someone is still an active member of the same community.

Two technologies coming out of the Internet2 Middleware initiative, Shibboleth (Cantor, 2003) and OpenSAML ("OpenSAML," 2003), are designed to help support assertions of trust between institutions without the risks of application-based passwords. Such tools will be central components in the emerging technology of Web services.

Conclusion

Although this chapter touched briefly on a number of issues, it should be clear that IT security affects almost everything we do at our institution. If your institution is connected to the Internet, you can never be 100 percent secure. IT leaders, especially chief information officers (CIOs), play a critical role in developing their campus IT security architecture. CIOs need to work with their IT staff and other campus leaders to understand the local security risks and define priorities for their management.

Another leadership role of CIOs is to strongly encourage their entire staff to take an active and consistent interest in security.

Every CIO needs to ask his or her staff to prove how well they are doing in securing the institutional IT infrastructure. If no one knows the answers or cannot provide corroborating data, it is time to pull together your team and implement plans to answer them. Ask your team questions such as these:

- Who tracks security vulnerabilities?

- Who is responsible for making sure that machines with vulnerabilities get fixed? How do we know they actually did get fixed?

- How do we plan to secure wireless access?

- How do we protect ourselves from attacks that occur within our campus network?

- How many accounts and passwords do people have? Do we feel that people use good passwords?

Finally, the IT leader must find ways to incorporate security into the funding and implementation of both new and existing projects. Portals, enterprise resource planning, or course management systems are all major projects. Look for opportunities in their funding and implementation to enhance the security of the entire campus.

References

Barton, T., and others. "Middleware Business Case." [middleware.internet2.edu/earlyadopters/draft-internet2-ea-mw-business-case-00.pdf]. Oct. 2001.

Briney, A. "CYBER-Menace: Special Report on Growing Virus Problem." [www.infosecuritymag.com/2002/may/cybermenace.shtml]. May 2002.

"Bugtrak Mailing List Archive." [www.securityfocus.com/archive/1]. Mar. 2003.

Cantor, S. "Internet2 Shibboleth Project." [shibboleth.internet2.edu/]. Feb. 2003.

"The Center for Internet Security." [www.cisecurity.org]. Mar. 2003.

"CERT Advisory CA-2001–26 NIMDA Worm." [www.cert.org/advisories/CA-2001–26.html]. Sept. 2001.

Dors, N. "Internet2 Web Initial Sign-on Project." [middleware.internet2.edu/webiso]. Mar. 2003.

Dunn, J. "Security Applications for Cisco Netflow Data." [www.sans.org/rr/software/netflow.php]. July 2001.

Fraser, B. "RFC 2196—Site Security Handbook." [www.faqs.org/rfcs/rfc2196.html]. Sept. 1997.

Frasier, M. "Understanding Virtual Private Networks." [rr.sans.org/encryption/understanding_VPN.php]. Mar. 2002.

Gray, T. "Firewalls: Friend or Foe." [staff.washington.edu/gray/papers/fff-final.htm]. Jan. 2003.

Grimes, S. "IDS in the Trenches." [www.infosecuritymag.com/2002/sep/roundtable.shtml]. Sept. 2002.

Gwaltney, R. "Protecting the Next Generation Network—Distributed Firewalls." [www.sans.org/rr/firewall/next_gen.php]. Oct. 2001.

"Internet Security Systems." [www.iss.net]. Mar. 2003.

Klingenstein, K. "Internet2 Middleware Initiative." [middleware.internet2.edu]. Mar. 2003.

Kohl, J., and Neumann, C. "RFC 1510: The Kerberos Authentication Network Service V5." [ftp://ftp.isi.edu/in-notes/rfc1510.txt], also [web.mit.edu/kerberos.www]. Sept. 1993.

"Nmap—Network Mapping Software." [www.insecure.org/nmap]. Feb. 2003.

"OpenSAML—Open Source Security Markup Language." [www.opensaml.org]. Jan. 2003.

"The OpenSSL Project." [www.openssl.org]. Mar. 2003.

Postel, J., and others. "Internet Assigned Numbers Authority Port Assignments." [www.iana.org/assignments/port-numbers]. Mar. 2003.

Roesch, M. "Snort." [www.snort.org]. Feb. 2003.

"SAFE SQL Slammer Worm Attack Mitigation." [www.cisco.com/warp/public/cc/so/neso/sqso/worm_wp.htm]. Feb. 2003.

"San Diego Super Computer Security Advisory." [www.attrition.org/security/advisory/misc/sdsc/97.05.caltech]. Sept. 1997.

Semjanov, P. "Russian Password Crackers." [www.password-crackers.com/]. 2003.

"University of Colorado Encrypted Authentication Security Standards." [www.colorado.edu/its/security/encauth]. Jan. 2003.

"Wireless Security and VPN." [www.intel.com/ebusiness/pdf/prod/related_mobile/wp0230011.pdf]. Oct. 2001.

Yasin, R. "What Is Identity Management?" *InfoSecurity Magazine* [www.infosecuritymag.com/2002/apr/cover_casestudy.shtml]. Apr. 2002.

7

Campuswide Security Education and Awareness

Shirley Payne

The old adage "ignorance is bliss" does not hold up where IT security is concerned. To appreciate this, just listen in as a help desk staffer tells a tearful student that the only copy of his term paper (due that day) has been trashed by a computer virus and is unrecoverable. Or find yourself on the pointy end of the boss's edict that *you*, a technically challenged human resources manager, will be held personally accountable henceforth for all security breaches in your department.

The need has never been greater for individuals at all levels and across all segments of the institution to understand what security threats exist and what to do about them. But how do you develop an effective education and awareness program for a topic that is not considered to be particularly interesting by the average person? How can you help such wide and varied groups of people on your campus (including students, parents, campus administrators, and the faculty, to name just a few) to understand the role they play in campus security? In this chapter, I examine some approaches to developing security education and awareness programs by defining target audiences and their unique needs for information, discussing a variety of techniques and tips for delivering the information to each audience, and suggesting strategies you can use for continuous improvement of your institution's programs.

The Case for Security Education

First, let's talk about why a security education and awareness program is so important—even when putting it together takes a lot of time and energy. Experts generally agree that people are the greatest source of IT security problems. Statistics consistently show that the majority of security breaches are caused by insiders, and the damage they levy on their organizations can be much more severe than anything wrought by hackers on the other side of the world (Pescatore, 2002).

Many, if not most, insider breaches are caused neither by disgruntled employees nor by students intent on doing harm. The sources are often people who either

- Are not aware of the security threats

- Are wrongly relying on someone else to deal with them

- Are not adequately skilled to address them, or

- Simply feel they have more important things to do

Unfortunately, potential intruders are all too aware of this human vulnerability, and they take advantage of it in a big way. Higher education offers many examples of security incidents leading to confiscation of hardware by federal authorities, loss or corruption of critical research data, and worse. Some have garnered national attention, and most could have been prevented with better education. Education, though, can be devilishly hard to deliver when

- Few computer users acknowledge personal responsibility for security

- Many consider the issue too technically complex for them to understand

- Executive and middle managers often fail to compre-
  hend the business implications of poor security and
  consequently don't assign it a high priority

- Security budgets and staff are typically stretched to
  the limit

In the face of these obstacles, it is especially important that a security education and awareness program be finely focused and all possible resources be leveraged. So let's start by analyzing precisely what information needs to be conveyed, and to whom.

Target Audiences Within the Institution

The most critical messages and the most effective ways to convey them can vary greatly from one target audience to another. In many ways security education is a marketing campaign, and certain marketing principles apply: know the customers' needs, select the right products for them, tailor the sales method for each customer group, monitor sales results, and repackage the product if needed. The customers to consider typically include the groups discussed next.

Administration

Because boards of trustees, presidents, vice presidents, provosts, department heads, and deans define strategic direction, set priorities, and allocate resources, an education and awareness program is necessary to help them understand security threats to the institution, risks posed by these threats, and what can be done to mitigate unacceptable risks. When security is explained in familiar business terms, it sheds its technical mystique, and managers at all levels can understand where to place it in the overall picture of operating the institution.

Along with providing a business case for security, a program should establish the right expectations among managers. They must know that other institutions and industries have the same issues and that no organization can be 100 percent secure—despite all best efforts, new threats will continue to surface and will require new measures.

Students and Parents

Unless a mandate is enforced to configure all PCs alike, students will arrive on campus with a hodgepodge of computer brands, operating systems, and software applications. Few of these computers will be secure; when plugged into the institution's high-bandwidth network, some will be victimized by crackers literally within minutes. It is important, therefore, to provide students with basic instructions for securing these computers before they arrive on campus. Involving parents in the education process can be helpful.

Faculty and Staff

This group can be a special challenge because faculty and staff typically believe it is someone else's job to take care of security. Defining how security issues can affect them personally, outlining the specific steps they can take to prevent problems, and emphasizing their individual responsibility to take those steps is an effective approach here. Remember to include information about federal and state laws governing use and protection of data, such as the Family Educational Rights and Privacy Act. Staff will typically comply once they understand what is required of them. Faculty can best be reached by convincing them that safe computing won't detract from their work—but *unsafe* computing surely *will*.

Researchers

Research labs are happy hacker hunting grounds. Security breaches are frequent, yet grant proposals that include the need for super-powered servers and workstations continue to leave unaddressed the need for knowledgeable system administration. Hence, this critical job often falls to underskilled (and sometimes *unskilled*) graduate students. Educate researchers before they write proposals, clearly communicating what security measures are necessary and what the institution's overhead allotment for research allows them to contribute, if anything, to addressing these measures. Include managers and staff from sponsored program offices in this education campaign.

Health Care Professionals

The administrative computing environments of teaching hospitals are commonly more centrally controlled than is typical of university academic computing. Desktop operating systems and applications are likely to be locked down—hopefully in a secure manner—with servers administered by central IT staff. Education on basic security steps, such as keeping operating systems up to date, may be less important here; but providing guidelines for handling sensitive patient data is paramount. Always an important issue, this is now even more critical as new federal Health Insurance Portability and Accountability Act (HIPAA) regulations become law. Penalties for noncompliance are significant for hospitals as well as for individuals. HIPAA regulations require ongoing education programs that address sensitive data security and accountability.

Auditors, Campus Police, and Attorneys

The wise security director recognizes the importance of working arm in arm with the institution's internal auditors on many security strategies. The relationship can be effective, though, only if auditors fully understand IT security threats, risks, and appropriate remediation steps. Further, educating them on existing network-level security measures for the entire institution provides them with the broader context they need when auditing individual department situations.

Campus police are being faced more and more often with the need to investigate computer-related incidents. Like auditors, police assigned to these cases need a foundation of knowledge regarding threats and risks. They also must be familiar with cyber security law and must be aware of resources, such as computer logs, that are available to help them with investigations.

In-house attorneys can help with several aspects of the security program, such as policy development. Also, executive management often calls on them for advice on IT security and responsible use issues. Again, ensuring that these individuals have a good understanding of threats, risks, and steps being taken to reduce risks is helpful.

State and Federal Government Relations Staff

The trend toward newer, tougher state and federal security legislation may provide important levers to aid higher education in addressing security problems, but it could also require actions that run counter to institutional culture and missions. Public schools that are subject to close oversight by state government are especially vulnerable. Individuals charged with responsibility for government relations must be alerted to possible new regulations and their potential impact on the institution, so they can exert favorable influence on proposed legislation.

IT Staff

There is no aspect of IT work that doesn't concern security in some way. Computer account management, help desk support, database management, application development, network administration— all must be conducted with security in mind. People performing these duties must master security basics, and each must acquire additional knowledge relevant to his or her particular responsibilities. A security education program is not complete unless it addresses both the basic *and* the special training needs of technical staff.

Perhaps no group is in greater need of specialized attention than system administrators, who by virtue of their responsibilities can either foster or foil institutional security measures. These people almost universally desire to perform their functions in a secure manner; they just need to be shown how.

A wealth of specialized training materials and Web-based resources are available specifically targeted at IT staff members, and these should be incorporated into any security training program for this group of individuals. For example, the SANS (System Administration, Audit, Network, Security) Institute provides security professionals, auditors, system administrators, and network administrators with resources, such as news digests, research summaries, security alerts, and in-person and online training and certification programs (www.sans.org).

Similarly, the CERT Coordination Center at Carnegie Mellon University's Software Engineering Institute provides training and education for technical staff and management on topics such as creating and managing security incident response teams, improving network security, and responding to and analyzing incidents (www.cert.org).

Effective Delivery Methods

Definition of customer groups simplifies the next important tasks: tailoring the security message for each group, and selling it effectively.

Meeting Presentations and One-on-One Discussions

Perhaps the most effective, albeit labor-intensive, means of building security knowledge is simply to custom-tailor presentations to specific groups and individuals throughout the institution. Doing so provides the opportunity to address specific questions to a captive audience. In one-on-one discussions with executives, it's possible to place security issues in precisely the right context and to highlight key security concerns within each executive's purview.

Handbooks

Security handbooks can be used to introduce students, faculty, and staff to security concerns and their responsibilities for addressing those concerns. Handbooks can be provided in hardcopy to all new entering students and employees as part of their orientation programs, with electronic versions posted on the Web for ongoing reference.

Online Quizzes

Some institutions require that students and employees successfully complete an online quiz before receiving their computer accounts. The use of online quizzes can thereby encourage users to read their handbooks and can serve to highlight critical points. A quiz can also provide the means for formally capturing student and employee agreements to abide by the policies and procedures detailed in the handbook.

Security Web Site and Web Ads

The need to update information on security threats and counter-measures is constant, and the Web is an easy and inexpensive means of keeping this information fresh, as well as accessible. Most institutions provide some security materials on the Web, but this information is sometimes scattered across many Web pages, making it difficult to find. A security Web site acts as a clearinghouse for all security-related information, placing it at the fingertips of those who need it.

An effective technique for leading readers quickly to information most relevant to them is to organize the material by roles. A system administrator, for example, might be presented with one set of materials, an average desktop computer user with another, and a department head with yet another. A role-based security Web site also forces the designer to think about the unique needs of each target audience, which will help to more easily identify content gaps.

The Web can be leveraged in other ways as well. Web ads (not the pop-up kind, *please*) that promote tips for enhancing security can be quite effective when placed on well-traveled sites throughout the institution's Web space.

Security Alerts

Information about the latest viruses and worms should be incorporated into the security Web site. Given how quickly these destructive programs can spread, though, it is also useful to push virus and worm alerts out to the user community. Existing mail lists of willing recipients can be used to e-mail these alerts or a new subscribed mail list can be set up for this purpose. Alerts might also be posted to the institution's Internet newsgroups, and if the virus or worm is particularly nefarious, an alert posted on the institution's home page may be appropriate.

A challenge with alerts is to maintain the level of customer interest. Too many alerts, and people tune them out; too verbose, and people don't have time for them. Alerts should be used sparingly, be timely, convey only essential information, and eschew technical details.

Security Fairs, Conferences, Seminars, and Workshops

Shoehorning security information into preexisting events, such as new student orientations, is a relatively easy way to promote the topic. Events specifically focused on security, though, allow outreach to groups and individuals that might not otherwise be touched. A security fair that is co-located with a student dining hall, for instance, can provide good visibility among this busy group of users. Security conferences featuring high-profile speakers can draw faculty, administrative and IT staff, campus police, and others. Workshops on basic security topics are especially effective and appreciated by those motivated to learn more. And advanced technical seminars and workshops specifically aimed at system administrators and other IT staff are essential to every security education program.

Articles

Articles in popular institutional publications are perfect vessels for carrying security information out to people who would not ordinarily encounter it. With the federal government's Department of Homeland Security enjoying so much press coverage, editors will understand that general security is a timely topic, and the idea of highlighting cyber security can be quite appealing. They might even be convinced to devote an entire issue to the topic.

Handouts

Postcards and brochures that convey specific warnings and tips are inexpensive to produce in-house and can be used in a variety of settings, such as back-to-school events, new employee orientation sessions, and open houses. Handouts should be easy to carry, attention grabbing, and short.

Videos

A few institutions have used videos to draw attention to security issues. One uses a scenario format featuring two students talking about security. Another uses children to lampoon irresponsible computing behaviors. Given the number of issues that compete for attention with busy students and employees, videos that are brief and entertaining are an effective way to bring security into focus. These videos can be showcased at various events and piped to dorms and other locations via campus cable channels.

Security Topic in Broader Subject Courses

Incorporating the security topic into various preexisting courses is another effective strategy. A security component included in technical courses is almost always appropriate, but it also fits well into courses designed to train staff on administrative applications. As part of the training, it's a good practice to require staff to acknowledge formally, perhaps via a signed memo of understanding, their responsibilities for protecting data obtained through the use of administrative systems.

Communication Tips

Security is a hard sell. Let's review some techniques for serving up security information in a dish that's palatable to customers.

- *Take the message to the people*. If you wait for your audience to come to you, you'll be waiting a long time. Deliver the security message aggressively; use conventional means such as posters and handouts, but don't neglect mechanisms such as bus placards, local TV and radio talk shows, and newspaper promos.

- *Be consistent in the message*. Everyone engaged in delivering security education should speak with one voice. Package the content and delivery for varied audiences, but provide the same fundamental message.

- *Write to short attention spans*. Wherever possible, break the message into small bits. If an idea can't be conveyed in less than fifty words, it is too long. If you need to present six ideas, six postcards or Web ads are better than one long think piece.

- *Make the message real to each target audience*. All materials should reinforce the idea that "it could happen to you." Use scenarios and case histories that are realistic and interesting for the particular target audience.

- *Make it fun*. Humor can be really effective when it is done well.

- *Repeat, repeat, repeat*. Use different angles to restate the most important pieces of the message in multiple ways.

Keys to an Effective Education Program

Security education and awareness programs must be updated continually to keep pace with emerging threats. Even the sharpest campaigns eventually lose their effectiveness. Strive to maintain value and interest in your program by applying new approaches and resources.

Solicit Input in Determining Priorities

A security education and awareness program can cover all of the basics and still not get the biggest bang for the buck. Comparing the program content to a prioritized list of high-risk security areas may reveal significant gaps. For example, most research universities recognize security lapses in their research projects, but their education and awareness programs may not include specific advice for principal investigators. Soliciting input from departmental system administrators and their bosses—asking what would help them the most in securing the computing environments they manage—can yield a better understanding of needed program improvements. Help desk staff and internal auditors can also provide valuable guidance for future development, since they see security vulnerability almost every day.

Base Program on Strong, Clear Policies

Building an education and awareness program can highlight policy lacunae. Advice to "Do this" or "Do that" usually begs the questions "Why?" and "What happens if I don't?" Without good explanations and sanctions behind the advice, a program can go only so far toward changing undesirable behaviors. Strengthening a program may, therefore, require updating existing policies or introducing new policies that support what the program is trying to accomplish. It may also require obtaining the support of the most senior executives of an institution to make the policy stick.

Given the wide variation in policy implementations within our institutions, policies related to security may be found in other policy statements about acceptable use, computing and networking, or data administration, or they may be part of more discreet departmental policies. In any case, policies that deal with security should be robust and enforceable, and they should be clear about what actions are necessary on the part of the members of the community and why. When people understand that they are accountable, they are more apt to listen when told how to discharge their duties.

Good models exist for campus IT security policies, and many are available at the Web site for the EDUCAUSE/Cornell Institute for Computer Policy and Law (www.educause.edu/ICPL).

Tap Creative Talents Throughout the Institution

Education and awareness programs are likely to be powered mostly by central IT. Although technical staff must define the message, the talents of nontechnical people throughout the institution can be used to frame and deliver it. Public relations and communications staff are wonderful sources for new ideas, as are employees and graduate students who work in instructional technology and other fields. Media services within the institution, such as video production, may also be put to work for the program—if not for free, at least at a cost below that of commercial services.

Place IT Security in the Context of Broader Security and Personal Safety Issues

Although many people are fuzzy about the risks of cyberspace, they understand what it means to be generally secure and safe. Placing cyber security in the context of overall safety removes the mystique and disinterest usually associated with cyber security alone. Engaging the campus police in designing and conducting parts of your program helps tremendously to reinforce this notion, and allows police to leverage the program for their own education campaigns. Several institutions are doing this effectively today. The University of Maryland's Department of Public Safety, for example, routinely includes information about computer security, spam, laptop theft, and related subjects in its regular newsletters. Campus police departments at many other institutions devote entire sections of their Web sites to safety in cyberspace and include practical advice on topics such as scams, stalkers, viruses, and hoaxes. (For an example, see www.ou.edu/oupd/inetmenu.htm.)

Consider Outreach Beyond the Institution

Once a program is in place and functioning well, there is the opportunity (and arguably an obligation) to take your message beyond the walls of the institution to local citizens, police departments, local and state governments, K–12 institutions, and businesses. Addressing these target audiences will almost surely bring new issues and perspectives into focus for the institution, and these can be used to enrich the program in ways that benefit all.

Build Partnerships Within and Outside the Institution

In addition to campus police, other organizations in the institution may serve as allies. If the university has a teaching hospital, partnerships with offices there are likely to be essential. Federal HIPAA regulations mentioned earlier will not only exert a major impact on health care workers, but will also affect people throughout the institution who work with protected health information. Student health staff, employee counseling staff, and research teams are a few examples. A partnership between the academic and medical sides of the house will help ensure that these people receive consistent education that addresses broad security issues and HIPAA in a single package.

Consider partnerships with other entities as well. With cyber stalking generally on the rise, for instance, women's centers may wish to participate in your program to educate students and employees on the topic. Student organizations may also show interest.

Alliances outside the institution may also be feasible. Consider partnerships in which the school already participates, such as those with vendors, other schools, government entities, and professional associations. The University of Virginia, for example, partners with the Federal Bureau of Investigation (FBI) to operate the FBI Academy, which offers criminal justice education programs (www.scps.virginia.edu/departments/fbi.php). This institution was able to capitalize on the relationship to obtain field-experienced faculty to teach a computer forensics class to staff.

Leverage What Others Are Doing

Finally, programs can get a significant boost by taking advantage of what others are doing successfully. Higher education institutions enjoy a long tradition of sharing among themselves, and in the realm of security education and awareness, what works well for one will probably work well for another. For example, the Virginia Alliance for Secure Computing and Networking (vascan.org) was formed by four universities (George Mason University, James Madison University, the University of Virginia, and Virginia Polytechnic Institute and State University) to share their security tools, best practices, and services (including education and awareness programs) with others in that state. EDUCAUSE provides similar resources at the national level through the EDUCAUSE/Internet2 Computer and Network Security Task Force (see www.educause.edu/security).

U.S. government-provided information is another resource to tap. The recently formed U.S. Department of Homeland Security (www.dhs.gov/dhspublic) is expected to yield additional tools and best practices, and the National Institute for Standards and Technology Security Resource Center (csrc.nist.gov/ATE) has long offered awareness, training, and education guidelines.

University-based security research centers are also good sources for courses and educational material. Purdue University's Center for Education and Research in Information Assurance and Security (CERIAS; www.cerias.purdue.edu), for example, is a leading provider of excellent courses and resource material for a variety of audiences, including K–12 and home users. CERIAS also has an active research program that covers a wide range of security and information assurance topics, as well as a continuing education program for postsecondary education.

Conclusion

The techniques described in this chapter cannot alone resolve all security concerns on campus but must be an integral part of an overall plan for security that involves specific technical approaches, policy development, and education programs. Even the most effective education and awareness program can only enable us to stay abreast of new threats and to exercise due diligence in making computer users aware of them. Even this much, though, is critical. Given the rapid and continuous growth of cyber threats to our institutions, we can afford nothing less than a security education and awareness regimen that is persistent, pervasive, and compelling. To borrow from a popular bumper sticker: If you think education is expensive, try ignorance.

Reference

Pescatore, J. "High Profile Threats Show Insiders Do Most Damage." *Gartner First Take*, Nov. 26, 2002, p. 1.

Index

"IT Security Cookbook," 66
IT security. *See* Security
IT staff. *See* Security staff

J

Jacobson, H., 49
Joint Information Systems Committee, 63
Jopeck, E., 33

K

Kenneally, E., 51
Kerberos, 82–83
King, C. M., 63
Klingenstein, K., 83
Kohl, J., 82
Krebs, B., 56

L

Lake, P. F., 53–54
Leadership: security, 21–23; and security architecture, 86–87. *See also* Security staff
Legal liability. *See* Liability
Liability, 45–57; civil, 49; and cybersecurity insurance, 56; and facilitator university model, 53–55; and negligence law, 50–53; security conditions with potential for, 47–48; and team approach to risk management, 56–57
Libraries, privacy measures of, 5
Logging, 8, 11, 82

M

Mandia, K., 66
Marchany, R., 31
McIntyre, D. J., 52
McRobbie, M., 19
Meetings, for presenting security education, 95
Microsoft products, virus protection when using, 78–79
Middleware: defined, 83; security considerations with, 83–84

Mission, higher education, 2
Mission Continuity Planning (Qayoumi), 33
Murrell v. Mount St. Clare College, 52

N

National Association of College and Business Officers (NACUBO), risk assessment information, 33
National Infrastructure Protection Center (NIPC), risk assessment model, 33
National Institute for Standards and Technology Security Resource Center, 103
National Institute of Science and Technology (NIST), risk assessment information, 33
National Science Foundation, 6, 13n2, 86
National Strategy to Secure Cyberspace, xii, xvi–xviii, 16
Negligence law, 50–53; breach in, 50, 52–53; duty in, 50–51; and facilitator university model, 53–55; and foreseeable harm, 51–52; general principles of, 50
Network scanning utilities, 80
Network security: best practices for, 75–77; defined, 74
Neumann, C., 82
Nichols, R. K., 63
NIMDA worm virus, 79
"Nmap—Network Mapping Software," 80

O

Oblinger, D., 1
Olsen, F., 19
Online quizzes, for security education, 96
Openness, balancing security with, 16
"OpenSAML," 86
"The OpenSSL Project," 85